# Building the Best Offensive and Defensive Cyber Workforce

Volume I, Improving U.S. Air Force Training and Development

CHAITRA M. HARDISON, JULIA WHITAKER, DANIELLE BEAN, IVICA PAVISIC,
JENNA W. KRAMER, BRANDON CROSBY, LESLIE ADRIENNE PAYNE,
RYAN HABERMAN

Prepared for the Department of the Air Force
Approved for public release; distribution unlimited

 PROJECT AIR FORCE

For more information on this publication, visit **www.rand.org/t/RRA1056-1**.

**About RAND**

The RAND Corporation is a research organization that develops solutions to public policy challenges to help make communities throughout the world safer and more secure, healthier and more prosperous. RAND is nonprofit, nonpartisan, and committed to the public interest. To learn more about RAND, visit www.rand.org.

**Research Integrity**

Our mission to help improve policy and decisionmaking through research and analysis is enabled through our core values of quality and objectivity and our unwavering commitment to the highest level of integrity and ethical behavior. To help ensure our research and analysis are rigorous, objective, and nonpartisan, we subject our research publications to a robust and exacting quality-assurance process; avoid both the appearance and reality of financial and other conflicts of interest through staff training, project screening, and a policy of mandatory disclosure; and pursue transparency in our research engagements through our commitment to the open publication of our research findings and recommendations, disclosure of the source of funding of published research, and policies to ensure intellectual independence. For more information, visit www.rand.org/about/principles.

RAND's publications do not necessarily reflect the opinions of its research clients and sponsors.

Published by the RAND Corporation, Santa Monica, Calif.
© 2021 RAND Corporation
**RAND**® is a registered trademark.

Library of Congress Cataloging-in-Publication Data is available for this publication.

ISBN: 978-1-9774-0785-6

*Cover: Staff Sgt Devin Boyer/Air Force.*

# About This Report

The U.S. military's success in cyberwarfare hinges in part on the capabilities of the cyber personnel that the military brings to the fight. Given that cyberwarfare is considered a core element of the U.S. Air Force (USAF) mission and a core capability that USAF provides to combatant commanders, USAF needs to ensure that its personnel are trained and developed in a way that best suits the cyber mission. With this in mind, USAF has been looking for ways to revamp and improve the training and development of its offensive and defensive cyberwarfare workforce to develop the best fighting force possible. USAF is also cognizant of the importance of recruiting and retention in realizing the full potential of any training and development efforts and has sought to better understand some of the drivers of attraction to and retention in the cyber field.

This report, the first of two volumes, summarizes RAND Project AIR FORCE's work exploring the views of the enlisted and civilian workforce on these topics. Our study builds upon similar recent RAND Corporation work focused on understanding the views of the officer cyber workforce (see Hardison et al., 2019). The results from this study will inform policymaker decisions about changes to USAF offensive and defensive cyber training and development efforts, as well as USAF efforts to recruit and retain the best personnel for the job. In this volume, we present our findings on training and development; in Volume II, we present our findings on recruiting and retention (Hardison et al., 2021). Some of the material presented in this volume—such as the impetus for our research and our overall approach—is repeated in Hardison et al., 2021. This report should interest cyber community leadership, USAF and U.S. Department of Defense leaders concerned with the management of the cyber workforce and the effectiveness of the cyber warfare mission more broadly, and USAF and U.S. Department of Defense senior leaders responsible for managing USAF career fields.

The research reported here was commissioned by the Secretary of the Air Force, Office of the Assistant Deputy Chief Information Officer for Digital Transformation and Assistant Deputy Chief of Staff for Cyber Effects Operations, and conducted within the Workforce, Development, and Health Program of RAND Project AIR FORCE as part of a fiscal year 2019 project, *Building and Retaining a Military Cyber Force*.

## RAND Project AIR FORCE

RAND Project AIR FORCE (PAF), a division of the RAND Corporation, is the Department of the Air Force's (DAF's) federally funded research and development center for studies and analyses, supporting both the United States Air Force and the United States Space Force. PAF provides the DAF with independent analyses of policy alternatives affecting the development, employment, combat readiness, and support of current and future air, space, and cyber forces. Research is conducted in four programs: Strategy and Doctrine; Force Modernization and Employment; Workforce, Development, and Health; and Resource Management. The research reported here was prepared under contract FA7014-16-D-1000.

Additional information about PAF is available on our website: www.rand.org/paf/

This report documents work originally shared with the DAF on September 26, 2019. The draft report, issued on September 30, 2019, was reviewed by formal peer reviewers and DAF subject-matter experts.

# Contents

# Figures

# Tables

# Summary

## Issue

The U.S. Air Force (USAF) has been looking for ways to revamp and improve the training and development of its cyberwarfare workforce to develop the best fighting force possible. As part of this effort, USAF expressed interest in better understanding the perspectives of the workforce, whose insights could inform further steps to improve training. Prior RAND work explored these issues among officers; this report focuses on the enlisted and civilian cyber workforces.

## Approach

We conducted 30 focus groups and interviews to collect viewpoints of enlisted and civilian cyber personnel in offensive and defensive cyber operations—specifically, the cyber warfare operations (1B4) specialty, digital network analyst (1N4A) specialty, and civilians operating as part of the cyber mission force. We also talked to leadership at the bases we visited and subject-matter experts in cyber workforce training and development. Figure S.1 shows participants' viewpoints.

## Conclusions

- Members of the cyber workforce and subject-matter experts acknowledged that there is room for improvement in training, and, according to some, major improvements are needed.
- Far more flexibility is needed in how cyber training is structured and delivered to ensure currency and to tailor training to the needs of the workforce.

## Recommendations

We grouped our recommendations into two categories, shown in Table S.1.

**Table S.1. Recommendations**

| Resource Changes | Structural and Cultural Changes |
|---|---|
| Would require additional human or monetary resources or shifting around of current resources | May require resource changes but also require structural or cultural changes |
| <ul><li>Develop and proliferate more training simulations and ranges.</li><li>Find new ways to test cyber capabilities using live red forces, but do so selectively.</li></ul> | <ul><li>Redesign training to be flexible and responsive to just-in-time needs and tailored to airmen's existing capabilities.</li></ul> |

| Resource Changes | Structural and Cultural Changes |
|---|---|
| • Institute cyber aptitude screening.<br>• Create an online forum for learning, information-sharing, and talent management.<br>• Provide more structure and oversight of trainings developed by individual units. | • Create senior technical roles that are not management oriented.<br>• Better educate the entire Air Force about what the cyber workforce does and how that work fits into the bigger USAF mission.<br>• Hire and retain experienced instructors. |

NOTE: *Live red forces* refers to live exercises that allow USAF personnel to practice engaging enemy forces by fighting against each other. The personnel engaging the enemy are *blue forces*; enemy forces are *red forces*.

### Figure S.1. Summary of Training Issues Raised by Participants During Focus Group Discussions

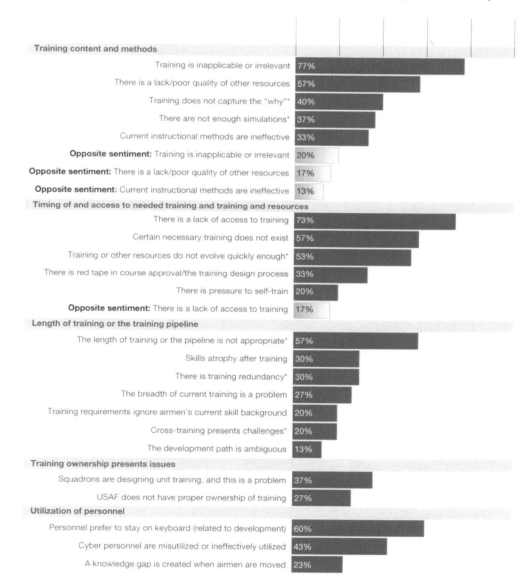

NOTE: We asked participants which aspects of training and development in their career fields needed to be improved and why. This figure details the variety of comments. Some focus groups had only one participant, meaning that they were essentially interviews. These interviews are included in the focus group results shown in this figure. When an *opposite sentiment* was expressed in more than 7 percent of the workforce discussions, it was added to the figure. Opposite sentiments are views that either run directly counter to the comments expressed by other participants or reflect someone noting or offering potential cons or downsides to a sentiment. Where an opposite sentiment was expressed in 3 to 7 percent of the workforce focus groups (i.e., one or two groups), the category is marked with an asterisk.

# Acknowledgments

We would like to acknowledge several people who contributed to this work. First, we thank Maj Gen Kevin Kennedy, Assistant Deputy Chief Information Officer for Digital Transformation and Assistant Deputy Chief of Staff for Cyber Effects Operations, for his guidance and input over the course of the project. We thank our study point of contact, Col Bobby Thompson, for his insights and assistance in developing and scoping the work. We also thank Danielle Vann and Lt Col Mary King from our sponsor's office for their assistance in identifying and contacting the various training subject-matter experts (SMEs) who participated in our study.

We are grateful to several key individuals at the RAND Corporation who contributed to the study. Sarah Soliman, an integral member of the team, contributed ideas over the course of the project, led focus groups at one of the military bases, and participated in several of the SME discussions. Col Katrina (KT) Terry, who also served as an important member of the team, assisted in the project during her year serving as an Air Force Fellow at RAND by participating in team meetings and offering feedback on the questionnaire items, the focus group discussion questions, the SMEs and bases being targeted, and other aspects of the overall study design and scope. In addition, we thank our peer reviewers, Caolionn O'Connell, Jeffrey Kendall, and Maria Lytell.

Lastly, and most importantly, this study would not have been possible without the assistance from our base points of contact and the participants themselves. Our base points of contact graciously gave their time to plan out and coordinate the visits, scheduled conference rooms for us to hold our discussions, reached out to members of the workforce to let them know about the focus groups and to encourage participation, and checked in on and escorted us as needed throughout our visits. It is because of them that our visits were successful. We are also grateful to all of the people who volunteered to participate in our study (SMEs and workforce members alike) and took time out of their busy schedules to share their views on the workforce's training challenges.

# Abbreviations

| | |
|---|---|
| ACC | Air Combat Command |
| AETC | Air Education and Training Command |
| AF/A1 | Deputy Chief of Staff for Manpower, Personnel and Services |
| AFB | Air Force Base |
| AFOQT | Air Force Officer Qualifying Test |
| AFS | Air Force specialty |
| AFSC | Air Force Specialty Code |
| ASVAB | Armed Services Vocational Aptitude Battery |
| CBT | computer-based training |
| CMF | cyber mission force |
| CNOQC | Computer Network Operations Qualification Course |
| CT | cyber test |
| CTAG | Cryptologic Training Advisory Group |
| CWO | cyber warfare operations |
| CYBERCOM | U.S. Cyber Command |
| DCO | defensive cyber operations |
| DoD | U.S. Department of Defense |
| DoDIN | Department of Defense Information Network |
| EA | exploitation analyst |
| FTU | formal training unit |
| FY | fiscal year |
| INWT | Intermediate Network Warfare Training |
| IQT | initial qualification training |
| IST | initial skills training |
| IT | information technology |

| | |
|---|---|
| JBSA | Joint Base San Antonio |
| JCAC | Joint Cyber Analysis Course |
| KSA | knowledge, skills, and abilities |
| KSAO | knowledge, skills, abilities, and other characteristics |
| MAJCOM | major command |
| NSA | National Security Agency |
| OCO | offensive cyber operations |
| PCS | permanent change of station |
| RIOT | Remote Interactive Operator Training |
| SME | subject-matter expert |
| SNCO | senior noncommissioned officer |
| TAPAS | Tailored Adaptive Personality Assessment |
| TDY | temporary duty |
| UCT | undergraduate cyber training |
| USAF | U.S. Air Force |

# 1. Introduction

The U.S. military's success in cyberwarfare hinges in part on the capabilities of the cyber personnel that the U.S. military brings to the fight. Given that cyberwarfare is considered a core element of the U.S. Air Force (USAF) mission and a core capability that USAF provides to combatant commanders, USAF needs to ensure that its personnel are trained and developed in a way that best suits the cyber mission. With this in mind, USAF has been looking for ways to revamp and improve the training and development of its offensive and defensive cyberwarfare workforce to develop the best fighting force possible. USAF is also cognizant of the importance of recruiting and retention in realizing the full potential of any training and development efforts and has sought to better understand some of the drivers of attraction to and retention in the cyber field.[1]

This report, the first of two volumes, summarizes RAND Project AIR FORCE's work exploring the views of the enlisted and civilian workforce on these topics. Prior RAND Corporation research explored these issues among officers (see Hardison et al., 2019).[2] The results of our study are intended to inform policymaker decisions about changes to USAF offensive and defensive cyber training and development efforts, as well as USAF efforts to recruit and retain the best personnel for the job. In this volume, we present our findings on training and development; in Volume II, we present our results on recruiting and retention.

---

[1] This section also appears in Hardison et al., 2021.

[2] Note that the cyber workforce community encompasses a much larger set of personnel than just those explored in this study. Within USAF, the cyber workforce includes additional enlisted career fields, such as the 3DXs (the cyberspace support career fields), officers, other members of the civilian workforce, and USAF reserve and guard personnel. Unfortunately, because of resource constraints, we were unable to explore all of these workforces in this study. Instead, to fit within our study budget, the sponsor scoped this effort to focus just on active-duty 1N4As (digital network analysts) and 1B4s (cyber warfare operations personnel).

However, the sponsor also acknowledged that there was interest in exploring these issues in the reserve and guard communities and in the other enlisted career fields (such as the 3DXs) and that there would be benefits in doing so. In addition, a view of these issues with the total force in mind might provide different insights and solutions. For example, the ability for reservists and guardsmen to work in the private-sector cyber field, attain additional certifications, and stay technically current while still having the opportunity to engage in military offensive cyber operations (OCO)–type work might be especially attractive for some personnel.

Lastly, it is worth noting that the study was scoped to focus only on training and recruiting issues in USAF but much of the cyber work and training being conducted exist in a joint environment, and many of the issues might be shared across the services. Therefore, a joint view of these issues could be worthwhile. Although we approach enlisted cyber workforce issues in this report from a USAF perspective only, these issues are in fact U.S. Department of Defense (DoD)–wide challenges. Given the joint, interagency, allied, and coalition operating environments that depend on cyber as a crosscutting domain, this force-wide view might be especially important in understanding cyber workforce issues.

## Why Training and Development Changes Are Needed

USAF interest in revamping training and attention to recruitment and retention is a response in part to recognition within and outside USAF that changes are needed in how the cyber workforce is managed and developed. The need for change has been highlighted in several recent studies (see, for example, Chiaramonte, Howe, and Collins, 2016; Hardison et al., 2019; and U.S. Government Accountability Office, 2019).

However, in the past, complexities in the development of the cyber workforce have presented challenges to achieving this goal, and some of these challenges are likely to continue to varying extents, at least in the near future. One challenge is that the cyber landscape has experienced profound growth and substantive changes in sophistication and complexity in recent years. As a result, the use of cyber on the battlefield and the associated demands for skilled personnel have also changed rapidly. USAF has continued to explore how best to manage this new and evolving cyber enterprise and its corresponding workforce, and the need to revisit workforce training and development is one piece of this evolution.

A second complicating factor involves the many career fields that make up the enlisted and civilian cyber workforces (including nine separate Air Force specialties [AFSs] for enlisted personnel, as well as engineering, intelligence analysis, computer science, and more on the civilian side). In addition, several types of cyber work are being performed in USAF, each with its own requirements for technical expertise.

A third complicating factor is the variety of key stakeholders (i.e., Air University, 24th Air Force, Air Force Institute of Technology, Secretary of the Air Force/Chief Information Officer, Air Education and Training Command [AETC], Air Combat Command [ACC], squadron commanders, Deputy Chief of Staff for Manpower, Personnel and Services [AF/A1], and others[3]), each of whom likely has unique and important insights into training and the changes that are needed. Understanding the differences across stakeholder perspectives will be critical in ensuring that any policy changes are addressing that full variety of needs.

A fourth complicating factor is a change that is underway in how cyber work will be managed; personnel are being shifted to cyber mission force (CMF) and mission defense team constructs.[4] This includes moving away from traditional communication squadrons (i.e.,

---

[3] This includes stakeholders outside USAF, including U.S. Cyber Command (CYBERCOM) and the National Security Agency (NSA).

[4] The CMF consists of 133 teams serving DoD's cyber mission. These teams are organizationally part of CYBERCOM and include Cyber National Mission Force teams that "defend the nation by seeing adversary activity, blocking attacks, and maneuvering in cyberspace to defeat them," Cyber Combat Mission Force teams that "conduct military cyber operations in support of combatant commands," Cyber Protection Force teams that "defend the DOD information networks, protect priority missions, and prepare cyber forces for combat," and Cyber Support Teams that "provide analytic and planning support to National Mission and Combat Mission teams" (Theohary, 2018, p. 1). *Mission defense teams* are teams within USAF that provide "active defense at the base level" and "protect key cyber terrain at wing and below in order to deliver cyber-based mission assurance for unit's assigned missions and weapon systems" (Weggeman, 2018, p. 7).

squadrons focused on traditional information technology services and building and maintaining the DoD Information Network [DoDIN])[5] and moving toward cyber operations squadrons (i.e., squadrons focused on offensive and defensive cyber missions). These changes will occur slowly over several years, and how training needs might change while the transition is ongoing and once the transition is complete is not well understood.

## Goals of This Study

Maj Gen Kevin Kennedy (Assistant Deputy Chief Information Officer for Digital Transformation and Assistant Deputy Chief of Staff for Cyber Effects Operations) and his staff have already identified many ideas for changes to training and development that might be beneficial for improving the cyber workforce, many of which are in progress. However, General Kennedy has also noted that additional insights from the workforce in the field might be especially useful in helping shape and inform additional changes to training as they go forward. He turned to RAND Project AIR FORCE for assistance in gathering those insights.

We focused our efforts on exploring the workforce's views on the following broad questions:

- Is the training and development process that exists now working well for the cyber workforce? Is there a need for improvement?
- If cyber training and development need to be improved, how might training be changed to better address the workforce's training needs?
- What would be the ideal way to train and develop cyber personnel, and what obstacles, if any, might be preventing the cyber workforce from implementing that ideal?

We then offer options for changes to the training process that USAF could consider to help address the workforce's comments and views on areas for improvement.

## Our Study Approach

In discussion with our sponsor, we scoped this effort to focus on the enlisted and civilian cyber workforces.[6] At the sponsor's direction, we explored the OCO and defensive cyber operations (DCO) workforces, specifically personnel in the enlisted 1B4 (cyber warfare operations) and 1N4A (digital network analyst)[7] specialties who work in the OCO or DCO cyber

---

[5] These activities are referred to as *DoDIN operations*, which include designing, building, configuring, securing, operating, maintaining, and sustaining "DOD communications systems and networks across the entire DODIN" (Theohary, 2020, p. 1).

[6] This section also appears in Hardison et al., 2021.

[7] We use 1N4A in this report to refer to personnel in Air Force Specialty Code (AFSC) 1N4X1A (i.e., 1N4s who are in the A shred). A shred is used to split a career field into two separate tracks, where each track develops specialization in a different content area within the field. Shreds are represented as an additional digit at the end of an AFSC designated with a capital letter (e.g., some career fields have an A shred and a B shred).

domains.[8] Also included in the scope of our effort were all civilians operating as part of the CMF. Within the 1B and 1N4 career fields, personnel working to build and maintain various aspects of DoDIN (i.e., personnel whose roles are similar to an information technology [IT] workforce in the private sector) were not included in this study's scope.[9]

We excluded consideration of officers because officers were a focus of a similar research effort two years prior to this study, the results of which informed a number of recommendations that the sponsor's office was executing at the time in which this study was underway (see Hardison et al., 2019). In that same study, the enlisted and civilian workforces were mentioned by participants as additional groups whose viewpoints were also worth exploring, and both were of direct interest to the sponsor's office as groups on which more-systematic research would be worthwhile.

The bulk of our approach relied on focus groups to collect viewpoints from these cyber personnel on how best to improve their training and development. We also interviewed key USAF cyber training and development subject-matter experts (SMEs) and stakeholders (including the career-field managers, cyber training squadron commanders, and personnel overseeing cyber training at Air University and the U.S. Air Force Academy) to identify their views on how to improve the training of cyber personnel.[10]

We chose focus groups and interviews as our primary study approach because our sponsor was particularly interested in the views of the workforce on needed changes in training to inform next steps that USAF plans to take in this area. Focus groups can be especially useful for this type of research goal for two reasons. First, they are useful as an exploratory tool to capture a wide variety of ideas and viewpoints. Second, they allow deeper understanding of ideas because researchers can probe for more details and ask for additional explanation. This probing for additional information can be useful not only for gaining a richer understanding of ideas that have not been previously considered but also for clarifying issues that are known to leadership but that perhaps are not fully understood or have been misunderstood. In this way, focus groups

---

[8] It is important to note that the 1N4X1A career field is not under the functional authority of the study sponsor. 1N4X1A does not typically align under OCO/DCO, but rather as CMF missions, non-CMF USAF missions, and Combat Support Agency missions. DCO missions for 1N4X1A are limited. The study scope included only those 1B4X1 and 1N4X1A who are participating in the DCO and OCO missions. This reflects most of the 1B4 community but only a subset of the 1N4As.

[9] This should not be taken to suggest that the sponsor's office was not interested in improving training and development in the DoDIN workforce as well, but, because of funding constraints, we could focus on only a subset of the cyber workforce in this study.

[10] In addition to talking with USAF cyber SMEs, we had hoped to speak with cyber representatives from the other services. However, interviews external to USAF have to be approved through a separate set of offices within DoD, and that approval process would have exceeded our timeline for the project. However, we did interview a few RAND SMEs who have extensive expertise in cyber issues among the U.S. Army and U.S. Navy cyber workforces to determine whether there might be any notable insights or lessons learned by these other services that could help inform our recommendations to USAF. What we learned from those discussions suggested that the other services are facing similar challenges relating to recruiting, retention, and training of cyber personnel and that they, too, are still looking for answers to address those challenges. There were no additional notable insights from those discussions.

can provide both a variety of information and a depth of understanding of the issues that other approaches might not.

*Focus Group and Interview Participants and Questionnaire Respondents*

To collect data on the cyber workforce's views, we visited three military bases (Fort Meade, Maryland; Joint Base San Antonio [JBSA], Texas; and Scott Air Force Base, Illinois). These military bases were chosen because they reflect bases with high concentrations of 1B4s or 1N4As involved in OCO and DCO, which would provide a good overview of viewpoints in the career fields of interest. As shown in Table 1.1, these three bases account for the majority of 1B4s, and two of them account for more than half of the 1N4As.[11]

**Table 1.1. Distribution of Personnel in the 1N4A and 1B4 Career Fields**

| Base | Personnel | |
|---|---|---|
| | 1B4 | 1N4A |
| Grand total | 809 | 990 |
| **Bases visited** | | |
| Fort Meade | 74 | 266 |
| JBSA | 465 | 239 |
| Scott Air Force Base | 75 | 5 |
| Total | 614 | 510 |
| **Bases not visited** | | |
| Fort Gordon | 12 | 65 |
| Goodfellow Air Force Base | 0 | 138 |
| Hickam Air Force Base | 27 | 77 |
| Hurlburt Field | 18 | 6 |
| Keesler Air Force Base | 23 | 0 |
| Naval Air Station Pensacola Corry Station | 0 | 135 |
| Nellis Air Force Base | 19 | 4 |
| Peterson Air Force Base | 15 | 3 |
| Bases with fewer than ten 1B4s or 1N4As | 81 | 52 |
| Total | 195 | 480 |

NOTE: These data come from the authors' analysis of the September 30, 2019, monthly extract of the Military Personnel Data System.

We held a total of 30 focus group discussions or interviews with members of the workforce,[12] which included a total of 68 enlisted personnel and seven civilians. As shown in Figure 1.1, the

---

[11] Because of the complexities in trying to identify OCO and DCO civilians, we were not able to provide a similar table showing the distribution across bases for the civilian workforce.

[12] For simplicity's sake, we will use the term *focus group* throughout the report to refer to both focus groups and interviews (i.e., focus groups with one participant) with members of the cyber workforce. See Appendix E for more information on focus group participants.

number of discussions varied by location: 12 each at Fort Meade and JBSA, five at Scott Air Force Base, and one by phone with a participant who was stationed at another location.[13]

At each location, we held discussions separately by work role (OCO or DCO), by pay grade grouping (senior noncommissioned officer [SNCO] versus noncommissioned officer, GS-11/12/13 versus GS-14/15), and by specialty type (civilian, enlisted 1B4, and enlisted 1N4A). Discussions were approximately evenly split between OCO and DCO work roles, and the overwhelming majority of the discussions were with enlisted 1B4s. The number of participants per discussion varied, ranging from one to seven, but in most groups we had two to three participants. Table 1.2 shows the overall number of participants by type of group.[14]

---

[13] Note that a few discussions with participants were held by phone to accommodate participants who volunteered but were unavailable to meet with us during our visit.

[14] Note that the number of 1B4s and 1N4As who participated reflect close to 7 percent and 5 percent, respectively, of these populations at the three bases (see Table 1.1).

**Figure 1.1. Number of Focus Groups, by Base, Work Role, and Specialty**

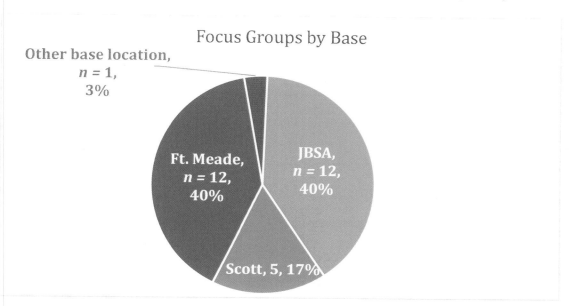

Focus Groups by Base

Other base location, *n* = 1, 3%

Ft. Meade, *n* = 12, 40%

JBSA, *n* = 12, 40%

Scott, 5, 17%

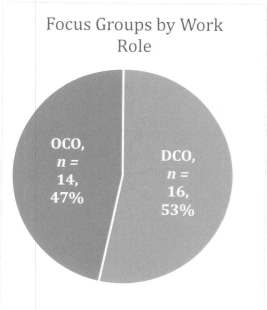

Focus Groups by Work Role

OCO, *n* = 14, 47%

DCO, *n* = 16, 53%

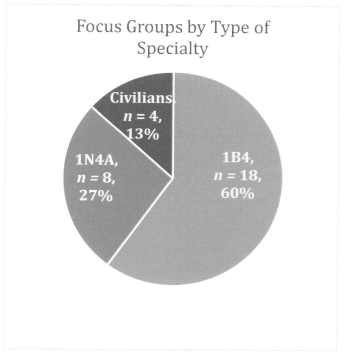

Focus Groups by Type of Specialty

Civilians, *n* = 4, 13%

1N4A, *n* = 8, 27%

1B4, *n* = 18, 60%

**Table 1.2. Total Number of Focus Group Participants**

| Type of Discussion | Number of Participants |
|---|---|
| By specialty | |
| 1B4 | 45 |
| 1N4A | 23 |
| Civilians | 7 |
| By work role | |
| DCO | 34 |
| OCO | 41 |
| By base[a] | |
| Fort Meade | 39 |
| JBSA | 17 |
| Scott Air Force Base | 18 |
| Total sample | 75 |

NOTES: Number per group is lower for JBSA in part because we held additional discussions by phone with a few participants who could not attend during our visit. Those phone discussions were held as interviews with one person per discussion.
[a] One phone interview participant was not located at any of the three bases we visited. The total number of participants at the three bases was 74.

During the focus group discussions, we administered a questionnaire that included both open-ended questions for write-in responses and questionnaire items to which participants responded using five-point Likert scales (i.e., strongly agree to strongly disagree).[15] Those items are explained throughout the report where those results are discussed. Our focus group discussions and questionnaire covered a variety of training topics:

- Are there gaps in knowledge, skills, abilities, and other characteristics (KSAOs) not addressed in training?
- What needs to be changed in training, and why?
- How might you change training if you could?
- Are there obstacles to improving training?
- Is there technology or equipment you need or need more of for training?

For more description on the questionnaire and the focus group content and participants, see Appendixes A and B.

In addition to the focus groups, we held a discussion at each base that included one or more leaders of cyber personnel (e.g., an officer, a superintendent, someone generally overseeing the

---

[15] We included some items that were similar to or identical to items used in other surveys of USAF personnel (e.g., the Federal Employee Viewpoint Survey and USAF climate surveys).

officer workforce). The goals of these discussions were threefold: (1) for us to provide background to them about the purpose and goals of the study, (2) for us to learn more about cyber and the cyber personnel at their base, and (3) for us to gather unique insights that they might have on the topics of training, recruiting, and retention. At one base, we held two such discussions; at the others, we held one.[16] These discussions were useful in that leadership's views contributed to some example comments provided throughout the report and to our understanding of the issues.[17] However, the figures presented throughout the report focus solely on the results from our discussions with cyber personnel.

We also held 12 discussions by phone with stakeholders and SMEs with knowledge and experience in training. As with the leadership discussions, we did not include their responses in the results presented in the figures throughout the report. However, their insights were useful in providing context about training that exists and about the career fields, and their views on what training is needed for the workforce were also useful. The SME and stakeholder participants and their insights are discussed in Appendix E.

We present our results in three ways. First, we present figures summarizing the number of focus groups during which particular comments about training issues or suggestions for changes were mentioned to give a sense of the relative frequency of a particular sentiment. For simplicity, we present these results as *overall* focus group percentages, regardless of whether the discussion was with 1B4s, 1N4As, or civilians (percentages within each specialty can be found in Appendix D).[18] Second, we intersperse results from our focus group questionnaire to provide further context on participants' views on these topics. Third, we provide comments that illustrate the variety of sentiments offered on these topics and note any differences in the comments observed across the specialties.

## Data Limitations and Implications

Several limitations to the data and results are important context for our findings and recommendations. First, the views of our focus group participants might not reflect the views of

---

[16] The number of discussions held was determined by leaders' availability. At one base, the relevant leadership participants were not available at the same time and therefore were scheduled for separate discussions.

[17] Leadership did not raise any notable issues that were not also raised by members of the workforce.

[18] We present responses together in the main body of the report for a few reasons. First, our sample size for civilians was too small to determine whether meaningful differences in viewpoints existed between the civilian and enlisted groups. In addition, the work performed by the civilian workforce is similar enough to that of the 1N4A and 1B4 workforces that their training challenges might not differ in many cases and any differences observed might be simply caused by chance because of the small sample sizes. We discuss this issue more in Appendix E. However, in discussing the comments, we do note any qualitative differences that we observed among the comments raised in the groups. Likewise, we note instances in which 1B4 and 1N4A comments were noticeably different from each other. The 1N4A sample size was larger than that of the civilians, but the number of focus groups (eight) was still too small to draw definitive conclusions about differences in the numbers of focus groups mentioning a topic. Therefore, we decided to report the overall focus group counts and address obvious differences in our discussion of the results.

the entire workforce because our participants come from select bases (not a random sample) and volunteered to participate.

Second, we largely assume that our participants' views are correct; however, it is possible that they could be inaccurate. For example, it is possible that training problems exist in different forms or to varying degrees from what was expressed by participants. With this in mind, leadership should consider whether additional data collection efforts might be needed prior to implementing a recommendation.

Third, our sample size for each specialty was small for all of the groups, but especially for the civilian workforce (seven participants in four discussions). Therefore, the results for that group, in particular, should be evaluated with strong caution because there are likely issues unique to that workforce that we were unable to capture or report.

Fourth, throughout the report, we present the proportion of groups in which at least one participant expressed a particular view or comment, and we discuss the comments in depth that were raised most frequently. However, it is important to point out that some comments might be widely held but still mentioned less frequently in focus group discussions because of the dynamics of the discussion. For example, not all participants respond to each question, and the discussion can quickly shift direction to other topics because of comments offered by other participants. In addition, some topics can be mentioned once, briefly, by one person in a discussion, whereas other comments might be discussed by all participants and reiterated multiple times during the focus group.[19] In this way, the comments mentioned by the largest proportion of groups might not always reflect the topics that participants feel most strongly about or the views that everyone holds. Therefore, the order of frequency that we present in our figures should be viewed with caution. That said, we also include the proportion of groups in which someone expressed an opposing viewpoint. This helps determine whether there tends to be disagreement with certain views.

Lastly, as we discuss further later, the 1B4 career field is cross-train-only, with personnel cross-training at different points in their careers. Because of this, it is possible that some of our more senior participants had been in the career field for a shorter period than some of the more junior participants. Although we did look at participant comments by grade to explore whether there were differences between more-senior and more-junior personnel, we did not split 1B4 participant comments out by length of time in the career field and therefore cannot tease out whether viewpoints by 1B4s differ notably by the number of years they have spent in the career field.

---

[19] Note that a topic mentioned briefly by one person could be a point with which everyone wholeheartedly agrees, and participants might choose not to add to it because they would just be repeating what the other participant has already said. In addition, a point that is discussed at length by participants might be discussed at length because the point is complicated and hard to explain, not because it is more important.

## Organization of This Report

This report provides an overview of our focus group findings.[20] In Chapter 2, we discuss participants' comments about whether changes to training are needed and provide figures summarizing the most frequently discussed training issues and solutions. In Chapters 3 through 7, we elaborate on the broad topics shown in those figures by discussing each specific concern or solution and providing examples of the comments that participants offered. In Chapter 8, we summarize the concerns raised by participants and present our recommendations for how to improve cyber training. These recommendations are based on our judgment of the most-promising suggestions that were offered by participants and on other recommendations that logically follow from participants' comments and from our knowledge and expertise in training and development of personnel but that might not have been directly suggested by anyone. Lastly, in Appendixes A through E, we provide additional focus group and interview data and results.

---

[20] As a reminder, Volume I focuses on results related to training and development of the workforce. Volume II focuses on results related to retention and recruiting.

# 2. Participants Report that Training Needs to Change

One main goal of our study was to help leadership identify ways to change training and development of cyber personnel to build the best cyber workforce possible.[21] For the purposes of our discussion, *training* was used to refer to any sort of training and development across the entire lifespan of someone's career, not just initial skills training (IST). That is, we used training broadly to refer to training, education,[22] and development that might be needed at the start of an individual's career (such as IST); training after an individual arrives at their first assignment (unit-specific training); continuation training or training to maintain currency that might be needed over an individual's career; and other relevant training and development that are needed to appropriately develop the cyber workforce.[23] We provided this expansive definition of training to our participants at the start of our focus group discussion about training and asked them to answer our questions about training with this expansive definition in mind.[24]

We asked several questions designed to prompt participants to provide us with ideas that would help inform training changes. One question, typically asked of participants at the start of the discussion, was whether there were any gaps in the workforce's KSAOs that were not being adequately addressed by training.

As shown in Figure 2.1, not all of the groups discussed this topic directly. In 67 percent of the discussions (i.e., 20 discussions), someone gave us a yes or no answer to this question. In other discussions, participants did not provide a direct response. In those discussions in which someone did provide a direct response, in the overwhelming majority (60 percent out of 67 percent, or 18 of the 20 discussions), at least one person said, yes, some KSAOs were not being adequately addressed. In only 10 percent of the discussions (three discussions), at least one

---

[21] We also explained that briefly exploring views on recruiting and retention was another goal of the study (discussed in Volume II) but that the bulk of our discussion would be focused on the topic of how to improve training.

[22] USAF typically talks about training and education as separate and distinct concepts; however, in practice, education and training are not always clearly distinguishable. In the cyber context, cyber courses likely include elements of both training and education.

[23] This definition is intended to include training that would be relevant to USAF cyber performance in joint assignments because many of the USAF cyber jobs performed by 1B4s and 1N4As are in joint environments (e.g., for CYBERCOM or NSA).

[24] We talked about retention and recruiting issues before starting the training discussion, so there is certainly a possibility that the discussion of retention and recruiting could have influenced the training discussion in some way. However, we did communicate to the participants before asking about retention and recruiting that training was going to be the bulk of our discussion and that we wanted to spend only a few minutes on the discussion of recruiting and retention. That explanation helped us quickly refocus the discussion onto the training topic. We opted to discuss retention and recruiting first to make sure that we could cover it quickly and would not run out of time at the end of the discussion to touch on it.

person offered the opposite view.[25] This result suggests that participants think that training could be improved.

Participants also offered follow-on comments, and many participants pointed out that one notable gap is associated with personnel being unprepared for the assignments that they have immediately following training. A few others added that KSAOs are, in some cases, assignment-specific, which means that it would be difficult to avoid training gaps without providing everyone with assignment-specific training. Appendix F provides examples of the specific comments that participants offered.

**Figure 2.1. Percentage of Focus Groups Commenting About KSAO Training Gaps**

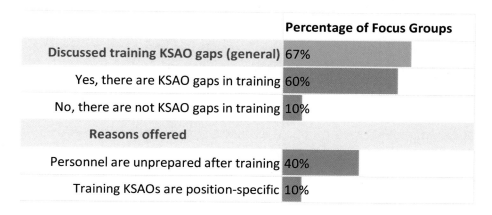

NOTE: Percentages represent the number of focus groups out of the 30 total in which a topic was mentioned by at least one person.

Questionnaire responses provide additional insights into how much improvement is needed. Two items that directly relate to the topic of training gaps are shown in Figure 2.2. This figure shows that participants responded neutrally on the topic of whether training prepared them for the responsibilities of the specialty overall,[26] and participants, on average, agreed that training gaps exist that have led them to be unprepared for specific assignments.

---

[25] Note that in one discussion, both views (yes and no) were expressed.

[26] Note that civilians' agreement is higher than that of the 1B4s and 1N4As on this question; however, given the small sample size for civilians, we cannot know whether this difference is real or just due to chance variation that would be caused by the small sample size.

**Figure 2.2. Average Responses to Questionnaire Items on Training Gaps**

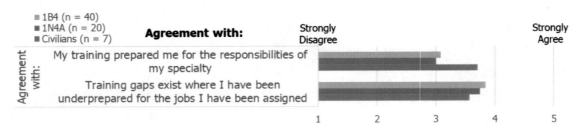

Other questions also helped clarify how concerned participants appear to be about training and how strongly they state that improvements need to be made. For example, Figure 2.3 shows participants' expressed views about job performance in their career field's workforce. The last item in the figure shows that participants, on average, rated the workforce's performance to be between fair and good. On the one hand, this suggests that they are not concerned about poor performance. But, on the other hand, it suggests that they think the workforce's performance could be much better than it currently is.

The other items show that participants expressed only slight agreement that the workforce is successful at accomplishing its mission. They also showed slight disagreement that the workforce is performing well relative to the private sector. They were slightly more positive about their performance relative to other career fields.[27] Taken together, these responses suggest that participants have higher expectations for performance in their career field than in others and that they do not rate the career field's performance as poor, but these results also suggest that participants expect the workforce's performance to be better and see plenty of room for improvement. However, it is important to note that job performance is a function of more than just training (e.g., motivation, underlying ability, and organizational constraints can also affect performance). Therefore, training might not always be the solution to addressing performance deficits.

---

[27] This is a subjective question that is asked in other USAF surveys. It is intended to get a sense of personnel's perceptions of a career field's relative standing compared with others in USAF. In those other surveys, no explicit comparison group is provided to the survey taker, and, similarly, none was provided in our survey.

**Figure 2.3. Average Responses to Questions About Job Performance**

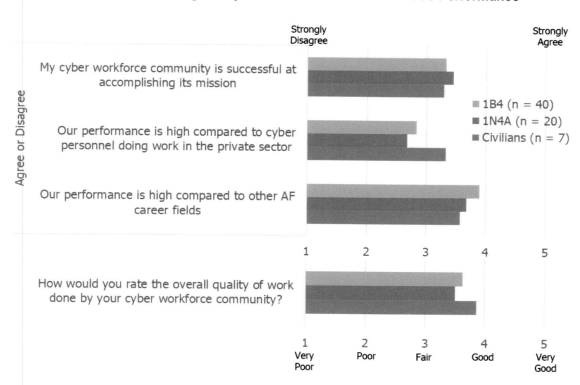

Figures 2.4 and 2.5 show that our participants' expressed views on how well training is preparing them are also not strongly positive and, in some cases, are even negative. As shown in Figure 2.4, 1B4 and 1N4A participants responded neutrally on whether they have the knowledge and skills to accomplish the mission and on whether the content of training is useful. They responded slightly more positively about opportunities to improve their skills, and they disagreed slightly, on average, that they have sufficient resources for training. But the most striking finding in Figure 2.4 is that the 1B4 and 1N4A participants disagreed, on average, that the cyber training resources are up to date and that the training is able to keep pace with the changing nature of cyber. Note that responses by civilians are notably different on a few of these items, especially the item about being given a real opportunity to improve their own skills—to which civilians gave positive responses—and the item about being provided up-to-date resources—to which civilians gave neutral responses. However, it is worth noting again that, because of the small sample size for civilians, it is difficult to tell whether those differences are meaningful or just due to chance.

**Figure 2.4. Average Responses to Questions About Cyber Training**

Figure 2.5 expands on the areas of training that potentially need the most attention, showing that participants, on average, reported being satisfied with the quality and content of technical training but neutral about the quality and content of IST.[28] In addition, the 1B4s and 1N4As reported being somewhat dissatisfied with continuation training, while the civilians reported being satisfied with it. Responses to satisfaction with 5- and 7-level training were the most negative, and some participants mentioned during our discussions that that was in part because no 5- or 7-level training exists. However, participants also explained that it might be appropriate in the cyber domain not to have 5- or 7-level training, in part because of the constantly changing nature of the field. Therefore, the traditional apprentice-journeyman-master model used in most USAF career fields might not be appropriate for cyber. These responses also give us a sense of where there is the greatest room for improvement in cyber training and how much room for improvement exists in these areas.

These questionnaire results provide important context for the participant comments that are discussed in the remaining chapters of this report. They help clarify that participants, for the most part, do not seem to think that the cyber workforce training situation is dire—but they do not seem to be strongly positive about the situation, either. The responses suggest that participants do believe that major improvements can (and likely should) be made to ensure that the cyber mission is successful.

---

[28] Civilians reported being slightly more satisfied, but, again, because of small sample sizes, we are unable to say whether the differences are meaningful or simply due to chance.

**Figure 2.5. Average Responses to Questions About the Quality and Content of Cyber Training**

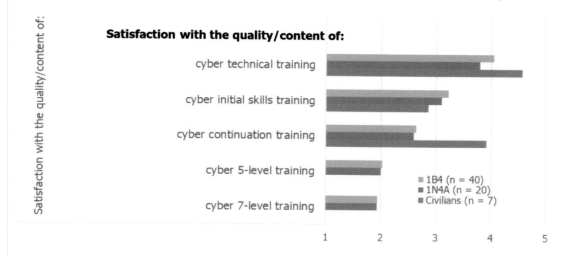

## Most Frequently Discussed Issues with Training

The remainder of this report summarizes the qualitative comments that participants offered during our focus group discussions. In the discussions, we asked participants to tell us which aspects of training and development (including initial skills and beyond) in their career field needed to be improved and why. Participants offered a variety of comments. Figure 2.6 displays comments mentioned in more than three groups (i.e., in more than 10 percent of the discussions).[29] As shown in the figure, several topics came up repeatedly across our focus group discussions: training content and methods, timing and access to training, training resources not keeping pace, length of the training pipeline, training ownership, and utilization of personnel. We grouped the comments according to these broad topic areas and discuss them in Chapters 3 through 6.

---

[29] We opted to establish an arbitrary cutoff of more than 10 percent (i.e., more than three groups) to help simplify the amount of information presented in the figures. Topics mentioned by three or fewer groups can be found in Appendix C.

**Figure 2.6. Views on What Needs to Be Improved in Training**

| | Percentage of Focus Groups |
|---|---|
| **Training Content and Methods** | |
| Training is inapplicable or irrelevant | 77% |
| Lack/poor quality of other resources | 57% |
| Training doesn't capture the "why"* | 40% |
| There are not enough simulations* | 37% |
| Current instruction methods are ineffective | 33% |
| Opposite Sentiment: Training is inapplicable or irrelevant | 20% |
| Opposite Sentiment: Lack/poor quality of other resources | 17% |
| Opposite Sentiment: Current instruction methods are ineffective | 13% |
| **Timing of and Access to Needed Training AND Training and Resources Are Not Keeping Pace With Cyber** | |
| Lack of access to training | 73% |
| Certain necessary training does not exist | 57% |
| Training or other resources do not evolve quickly enough* | 53% |
| Administrative red tape in course approval/training design process | 33% |
| There is a pressure to self-train | 20% |
| Opposite Sentiment: Lack of access to training | 17% |
| **Length of Training or Training Pipeline Is Not Appropriate** | |
| Length of training or the pipeline is not appropriate* | 57% |
| Skills atrophy after training | 30% |
| Training redundancy* | 30% |
| Breadth of current training is a problem | 27% |
| Training requirements ignore airmen's current skill background | 20% |
| Cross-training presents challenges* | 20% |
| Development path is ambiguous | 13% |
| **Training Ownership Presents Issues** | |
| Squadrons are designing unit training and this is a problem | 37% |
| The Air Force does not have proper ownership of training | 27% |
| **Utilization of Personnel** | |
| Personnel prefer to stay on keyboard (related to development) | 60% |
| Cyber personnel are misutilized or ineffectively utilized | 43% |
| Knowledge gap is created when airmen are moved | 23% |

NOTE: Sometimes, a topic was raised by one person and an opposite view was expressed by someone in the same discussion group. In those cases, the same discussion would be counted in both the topic frequency and the opposite sentiment frequency. For some topics, no opposite sentiment was expressed in the workforce discussions. Where an opposite sentiment was expressed in 3 to 7 percent of the workforce focus groups (i.e., one or two groups), the category is marked with an asterisk. In this figure, no opposite sentiments were expressed by 10 percent of focus groups (i.e., three groups). All percentages are out of a total of 30 discussions.

18

Figure 2.7 summarizes the most frequently mentioned ideas for training changes and solutions that were offered by our participants: suggested changes to training content and methods, ownership, and structure; the need for better instructors and applicant screening; and the suggestion to look to the other services for solutions.[30]

As with Figure 2.6, we include only those topics that were mentioned in more than three groups (i.e., more than 10 percent of the discussions). In cases in which the *suggested solutions* to training challenges align with the training *issues* (shown in Figure 2.6), we discuss them in the related chapter of this report. The cases in which the suggested solutions to training challenges do not align with the training issues are discussed in Chapter 7. In that chapter, we also briefly discuss some additional suggestions (not shown in Figure 2.6) mentioned in three or fewer groups.

In all cases in which we identified and coded for a type of a comment, we also coded for what we refer to in the figures as *opposite sentiments*. These are views expressed in the discussions that either run directly counter to the comments expressed by other participants or reflect someone noting or offering potential cons or downsides to a sentiment we coded. These *opposite sentiment* comments are flagged in Figures 2.6 and 2.7 and in other figures throughout the report to highlight when there was debate, inconsistency in views, or expression of potential downsides about a view.

In cases in which there was a modest number of groups expressing an opposite sentiment (more than 10 percent of groups), the comment is listed in the figure along with the proportion of groups expressing it. In cases in which the sentiment was expressed in 3 to 7 percent of groups (one or two groups), the sentiment is flagged with an asterisk (*); in cases in which the sentiment was expressed by 10 percent of groups (three groups), the sentiment is marked with two asterisks (**). In many cases, no opposite sentiment was expressed. For example, in Figure 2.7, although many participants said that more opportunities for simulations and opportunities to practice against live red forces (which we also refer to as *live reds* or *live red simulations*)[31] would be beneficial, there were also caveats offered. Some participants commented that simulations would be of limited use if implemented poorly. Some commented that simulations would need to be very advanced and constantly kept up to date, which might not be feasible to do. Some also

---

[30] As a reminder, although we show the comments ordered by the proportion of groups mentioning them, it is important to point out that some comments might be widely held but still mentioned less frequently in focus group discussions because of the dynamics of the discussion. For example, not all participants respond to each question, and the discussion can quickly shift direction to other topics because of comments offered by other participants. Therefore, order of frequency should be viewed with caution.

[31] *Live red forces* refer to red flag–type exercises in which combat forces engage in realistic, live training scenarios that allow USAF personnel the opportunity to practice engaging enemy forces by fighting against each other. In these scenarios, the personnel engaging the enemy are known as *blue forces*, and those fighting against them are *red forces*. *Simulations*, or *sims*, refer to the use of training ranges to simulate various cyber scenarios for training purposes. These simulations do not typically involve the use of a live adversary. They are more akin to a flight simulator that allows repeated practice of the same set of predetermined scenarios. These ranges can also be used to test new approaches and technologies in a secure environment.

commented that fully implementing cyber practice opportunities in the setting of a live red simulation would not be ideal, because doing so could effectively shut down the entire exercise, which would prevent the other participating groups (e.g., pilots and special-tactics personnel) from benefiting from it. Opposite sentiments like these are also explained and discussed in the chapters that follow.

**Figure 2.7. Cyber Workforce's Suggested Training Solutions and Changes**

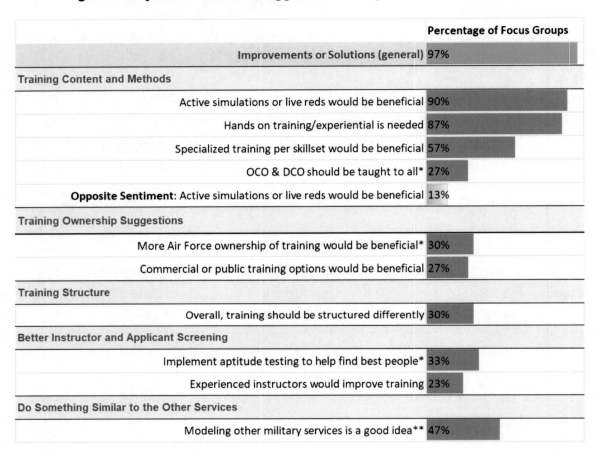

NOTE: Sometimes, a topic was raised by one person and an opposite view was expressed by someone in the same discussion group. In those cases, the same discussion would be counted in both the topic frequency and the opposite sentiment frequency. For some topics, no opposite sentiment was expressed in the workforce discussions. Where an opposite sentiment was expressed in 3 to 7 percent of the workforce focus groups (i.e., one or two groups), the category is marked with an asterisk. Where an opposite sentiment was expressed by 10 percent of focus groups (i.e., three groups), the category is marked with two asterisks. All percentages are out of a total of 30 discussions.

# 3. Training Content and Methods

This chapter provides participants' comments about the first broad topic area: issues with training content and methods. Figure 3.1 shows the issues that were raised by participants in more than three focus groups. In the sections that follow, we discuss each of these issues. Figure 3.2 shows solutions to improve the training content that were offered in four or more groups. We discuss these solutions and changes later in the report, when these topics are raised in the discussion of the related issues. In this chapter and in later chapters, quotations from interviewees refer to several schoolhouses: NSA refers to the NSA Cryptologic School (the school owned and operated by the NSA) and courses offered in the school course catalog, Keesler refers to 1B4X1 IST, and Hurlburt refers to initial qualification training (IQT) (1B4X1, 1N4A, or civilian). For a list of the various training courses completed by 1B4s and 1N4As (many of which are referenced in our participant comments), see Appendix G.

**Figure 3.1. What Needs to Be Improved in Training: Training Content and Methods**

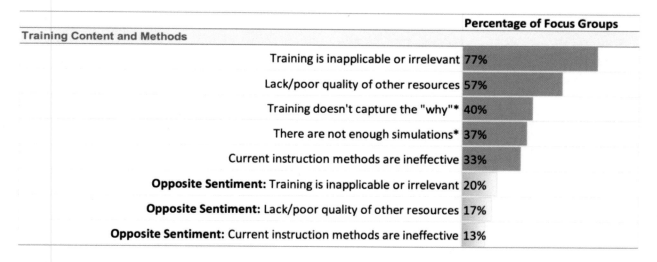

NOTE: For some topics, no opposite sentiment was expressed in the workforce discussions. Where an opposite sentiment was expressed in 3 to 7 percent of the workforce focus groups (i.e., one or two groups), the category is marked with an asterisk. Percentages represent the number of focus groups in which a topic was mentioned by at least one person. All percentages are out of a total of 30 discussions.

**Figure 3.2. Workforce's Suggested Training Solutions and Changes: Training Content and Methods and Instructors**

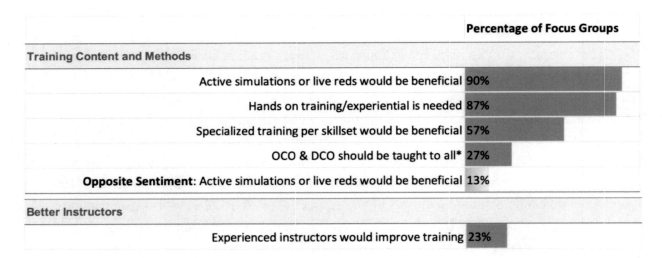

| | Percentage of Focus Groups |
|---|---|
| **Training Content and Methods** | |
| Active simulations or live reds would be beneficial | 90% |
| Hands on training/experiential is needed | 87% |
| Specialized training per skillset would be beneficial | 57% |
| OCO & DCO should be taught to all* | 27% |
| **Opposite Sentiment**: Active simulations or live reds would be beneficial | 13% |
| **Better Instructors** | |
| Experienced instructors would improve training | 23% |

NOTE: Sometimes, a topic was raised by one person and an opposite view was expressed by someone in the same discussion group. In those cases, the same discussion would be counted in both the topic frequency and the opposite sentiment frequency. For some topics, no opposite sentiment was expressed in the workforce discussions. Where an opposite sentiment was expressed in 3 to 7 percent of the workforce focus groups (i.e., one or two groups), the category is marked with an asterisk. Percentages represent the number of focus groups in which a topic was mentioned by at least one person. All percentages are out of a total of 30 discussions.

## Training Is Inapplicable or Irrelevant

As shown in Figure 3.1, in the vast majority of discussions (77 percent), focus group participants expressed general dissatisfaction with the applicability and relevancy of available training. For example, some training courses were described as courses that were needed for certain certifications or requirements but were not helpful and were regarded as a waste of time. Participants also discussed how courses within initial training and continuation training were often inadequate for certain cyber operator jobs. This overall sentiment was shared across our participants, with civilians and 1N4A and 1B4 airmen all commenting on the inapplicability of particular aspects of training.

Some participants talked about overall shortfalls in IST:

> In general, the training we are given is a good starting point, but it never really builds upon itself to help further our cyber skills. I've been through offensive and defensive [training] . . . now, CPT [cyber protection team] specific here as an example, and the training we are given to operate our weapons system is training to start it up. That is literally it; there is no training that actually teaches us how to use it properly. [1B4]

***

> Some of the challenges . . . [occur because] Keesler is a one-size-fits-all monkey, [and airmen are] trained to a lower level than they should be. They go to unit, and the unit has to spend a ton of time continuing training them. [Civilian]

***

> What we are lacking in our training is the two most important skills in cyber . . . automation and scalability. We are working on networks of various sizes, and to be able to scale up to any size of network in an automated manner is crucial to being effective. Our initial training does not teach that. Does that need to be in initial training? Probably, but it doesn't teach that. [1B4]

Some participants talked about specific courses:

> I feel like JCAC [Joint Cyber Analysis Course] is a waste of time. It's all memorization. Very little hands-on. When I went through in 2014, I wrote that—JCAC is basic stuff, but, in order to make an analyst, make them go through hacker courses. That builds them up more, knowing what the operations system does. [1N4A]

***

> CWO [cyber warfare operations course, IQT]—I'll call that the advanced course—that course definitely needs some work. It's defensively focused. You need to put people in training respective to where they're going to go. There are similarities between the mission sets of OCO and DCO, but . . . I do not view that course as adequate as an initial qualification training to come to an offensive site. [1B4]

However, an SME who reviewed our report noted that JCAC was revised significantly in 2015, after the above participant completed it. It is therefore possible that the participant's complaints about the course have already been addressed.[32] This same comment (that training may have been updated or improved already) could apply to any courses about which our participants expressed concerns, given that many of our participants had completed these courses some number of years ago.

Some participants talked about how private-sector training was not necessarily applicable in many cases.

> There are over 100 opportunities to go to a cyber training opportunity like a SANS [Institute] course or Cisco course. While that would help me be a [system] administrator or be great setting up routers or troubleshooting network problems, that can help the analyst, but it doesn't make us better analysts or cyber operators. [1N4A]

***

> A lot of these civilian side certifications . . . [and] models don't apply to how the military applies cyber in an actual environment. They don't have the bureaucracy that we have to go through. They can get from point A to B going through a network or whatever their objective is, and that is how they teach you within the confines of the class. But due to the restrictions placed on us by authorities, by

---

[32] A review of the JCAC curriculum is conducted every two years, and each service has a vote in the changes or modifications. This is done through a Cryptologic Training Advisory Group (CTAG) board. The CTAG report results in changes to the course.

the agency [NSA], a lot of that is not necessarily a one-for-one application. [1N4A]

Lastly, some participants talked about how the training system was broken and causing the lack of relevance.

> That's why I say just get people to mission. . . . the Air Force way of training is they send you to school and you learn everything you can there, but only that. Then, at the next school, they tell you to forget everything from the last school and learn only what we're teaching you. Then, you get to your unit, and they tell you to forget everything that you learned in training because it's all bull and out of date—this is the stuff you need to learn here. Then, you get to your actual shop, and they say to forget what your unit told you. Then, you go to another base, and it happens again. It takes 3.5 years to get through training, and, at every stage of the pipeline, this happens. That's how Air Force training goes. [1B4]

***

> If you have someone who is proactive, they will fight and hassle to get more training, but I don't know if that is a repeatable model for everyone in your unit. Some people are happy to just sit back and work with the training they have for the next three years unless there is an active development plan—some units have it, and some don't. [1N4A]

It is worth noting that some of these comments are about USAF-controlled courses and some are about courses that USAF does not control. For example, training at Keesler and CWO (IST) training are both provided by USAF. In these cases, USAF could implement direct changes to address the types of comments offered in this section and in subsequent sections of this report.

However, not all cyber courses given to USAF cyber personnel are under the control of USAF (see Appendix G). For example, some OCO training is an NSA requirement, and the courses are developed, managed, and provided by NSA. Therefore, USAF has no control over those NSA courses. Similarly, JCAC is a joint training class, run by the Navy and accredited by NSA. Therefore, USAF does not have much leverage to implement changes to JCAC, because USAF is only one service at the table. Lastly, some training, such as SANS Institute or Cisco training, is provided by private-sector companies and therefore also might not be changeable.

Nevertheless, even when courses are not changeable by USAF, these comments still might, in some cases, be useful in understanding what USAF could do to improve the overall training experience. For example, USAF could seek to better track which private-sector training and certifications might be rendered irrelevant because of the requirements levied on military personnel engaged in activities on NSA infrastructure. Better understanding and tracking of that could help determine for whom the training might be useful and for whom it would not.

The following are some examples of opposite views that were reported in 20 percent of the groups (see Figure 3.1):

> I enjoyed the training I received at Keesler AFB [Air Force Base], and I felt it helped me build a solid foundation for future education in the career field. [1B4]

***

[Training is relevant for the demands of cyber?] I believe so—at the least, the training courses I have taken. [1B4]

## There Is a Lack of or Poor Quality of Other Resources

In most discussions, participants mentioned a lack of sufficient or adequate resources needed for training. Participants generally discussed a lack of sufficient instructors, outdated or nonfunctioning materials, and inadequate funding. Furthermore, this issue was pervasive throughout specialties and career fields: 1N4As, 1B4s, and civilians all commented on being limited by resources.

One of the key resources for successful training is qualified and capable instructors. Unfortunately, participants frequently described USAF-provided training courses in which USAF instructors were ill equipped to effectively teach students about the skills necessary to be effective cyber operators.

> Some are just not good teachers, but you can see that versus a lack of knowledge and lack of experience. Getting that actual experience can help with not being a good teacher, so mostly just lack of experience. [1B4]

> \*\*\*

> A lot of times, you'll find in these pipelines that they take someone who is smart and put them in training. But they may not be the best instructors or want to teach or do the research so they do the course the right way. We don't look for the people with the right education mindset in those situations and make the decisions. [1B4]

> \*\*\*

> If you're particularly good at something, you could be adjunct faculty to help train or teach that class. I think that would help with availability of the actual training. [Civilian]

The sentiment of USAF instructors in the initial training pipeline being inadequate was shared among participants in many other discussions.

> I don't think they were proficient enough. I think I'm a better instructor than they are. Some didn't want to be there. I think some just sat in the back and let others teach. Some had the attitude, "Well, I'm the instructor, so you sit back and listen." Others rushed through material; if you raised your hand, they overlooked you. One didn't want to be an instructor. One said, "I had no idea what this material is, but I was told to teach it, so here we go through this PowerPoint." [1B4]

> \*\*\*

> I had more knowledge than some of the instructors; we were having to correct them sometimes. [1B4]

25

A particular point brought up by OCO cyber operators was the lack of instructors with an offensive focus. Because there are more defensive operators, some OCO participants noted that some instructors lacked the experience and expertise to effectively teach offensive training.

> I think from our OCO perspective, we have to invest in bodies. We need to send more resources, people with operational experience to go be instructors. [1B4]

***

> Having more educated instructors would be hugely beneficial. Most of them were defensive because that is the majority of my field. Not one of them knew about the offensive. . . . I had more knowledge than some of the instructors; we were having to correct them sometimes. Big thing is to have more knowledgeable instructors and having a variety of defensive, they've gone through defensive and know all of that, and also some people that are OCO that can help teach part of that as well. [1B4]

Other participants pointed out that it is difficult to get the most-qualified operators to volunteer to serve as instructors, in part because of concerns that their skills will atrophy, and, if forced to choose between the possibility of skills atrophying and leaving the service, many would separate. When asked for solutions, some participants suggested giving trainers and instructors better incentives to help encourage the most-experienced and the brightest operators to volunteer to instruct. Finding ways to get more-experienced instructors was mentioned as a solution by our participants in multiple groups (see Figure 3.2). These sentiments were also echoed in their responses on the questionnaire. As shown in Figure 3.3, participants in all three groups agreed or strongly agreed, on average, that the instructors with operational experience were valuable. (Other topics shown in Figure 3.3 are discussed in later sections.)

**Figure 3.3. Average Responses to Questions About Specific Training Features**

How valuable would the following be to include:

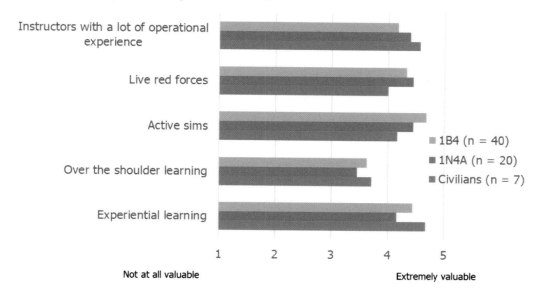

Along with effective teachers, cyber training requires various computer materials and systems. Participants discussed how these resources are often lacking—and, in certain situations, are either nonfunctional or frequently in need of repair and update. This was an issue found in both initial and continuation training. When discussing initial training, one participant stated,

> When I went through CWO [Apprentice Course, IST], half the course was broken. We had NetWars, a simulated network that we could go online and play around in, do forensics, attack and stuff like that, but it was down almost the entire course. We were actually supposed to do a test on that but were told, "Well, it's down, so we are just going to skip that test." That was the part I was most excited about the course because I can play around and do my own thing in there, but it was down most of the time. Having reliable training material would be good. [1B4]

Even when the materials are present and functional, the technology might be outdated, which can limit the effectiveness of the training.

> Depending on the mission, sometimes the Air Force network isn't current, and it isn't current to industry. I think the training depends on what you need. My units, I would say his unit is way behind the curve. They are using old tech; they are interfacing with a complex system that will not allow them to do what they need to do. So, when you talk about training, you are training on a mission with the tools they have, not what we really want to get it. [1N4A]

Participants also talked about how network issues can hinder cyber training.

> The biggest gap is our network. A lot of the training, some of it is not bad, but our network makes it unusable. It's slow, has a lot of security layers. When you are trying to run a simulator and it freezes every few seconds, you aren't getting

anything out of it. That is the worst aspect of training—it keeps us from getting any better. [1B4]

Although equipment and networks are both key to cyber training, participants also noted that many problems arise because of lack of funding. Often, participants noted that units and training courses were unable to purchase equipment or support cyber operator training because they lacked the necessary funding.

> We have some training ranges for in-house training. It comes down to money. We had this phenomenal lab, but they ran out of money and couldn't buy the licenses. And so now we rely on others to maintain the ranges, and that costs money . . . then, there are rules that limit our ability to use a range. If we want to do malware and want to watch what it does, we can't do that. We can't learn what it does and how to detect it. We can't do forensics on it. [1B4]
>
> ***
>
> Money, I've seen it be used as a rationale for why certain trainings don't exist. I don't know if I can tie it to one entity or unit in particular, but I've seen some units say they can't do training because they'll say they don't have enough money or seats to support the training. [1N4A]
>
> ***
>
> The CWO is a good course. It was designed well, but not everyone gets to take it. They are moving in the direction of making it mandatory for all of our members. Then, you take the weapons systems in detail, then it ends up we need a range to work on to rehearse those skills, and it isn't available. We need the manpower to create and set it up, and we don't have it. Our enlisted is busy with other things, though, and can't always set it up. [Civilian]
>
> ***
>
> As you start to run out of money, [technology needed for training] is one of the first things they start to cut back on. Two star something, we can do more because he can sign off on more. We are more limited as money runs dry. Early on in the year, tech gets cut as it goes on. [1N4A]

To address some of these issues, some participants (including some SMEs) suggested having more-dedicated personnel whose job is to advocate for, provide planning and oversight for, or design elements of training. Suggestions included adding an AETC cyber training wing at Keesler that would have dedicated cyber experts who could understand the cyber workforce's needs and advocate for them, similar to what is done for special forces. One participant explained, "When we are asking for funding, why would they fund something they don't understand?"

Others suggested creating a training-development cell whose job is to design ranges and expert training curricula and make adjustments to continually update them to keep pace with cyber. Participants expressed the view that with cyber, the training approach needs to be different from that used in other career fields because of the complexity of the work and the speed of changes in the field. They explained that, unlike instructors in other career fields, cyber instructors have to specialize in a single training block. In other career fields, instructors easily can and typically do instruct across multiple blocks. This means that the training curriculum itself is much more advanced. This also means that developing curricula is more complicated than it would be in other career fields, and instructors who teach full time do not have the time to build the level of curriculum that the career field deserves.

In addition, participants explained that in other career fields, the course material does not need to change much, if at all, for years because the material is static and unchanging (e.g., airplane engines do not change rapidly). As a result, there is no need in many other career fields to keep updating the training regularly to keep it current; once the curriculum is established, there is little additional tweaking needed. This is not so in the cyber field, which puts a much larger burden on the instructors who want and need the curriculum to be updated, changed, and even overhauled regularly. Instead, cyber career fields might need additional manning to address this difference. A separate, dedicated cell for developing and updating training equipment, software, and content could help address that need.

Lastly, some participants talked about how units have plenty of resources for training but IST does not get the same type of attention when it comes to resources. Participants explained that, to develop really good training, it would be helpful to have the assistance of academic experts (i.e., hiring computer scientists from the broader academic community) to help build out the courses. But participants noted that while the units could hire someone with that expertise to build out training in the field, the schoolhouses have no such ability.

The following are some examples of the comments that were coded as an opposite sentiment in this category (17 percent in Figure 3.1):

> [When asked if they saw a need for any additional technology or equipment for training] No—we have had everything we need. You really just need computer[s] and software and you can make it happen. We had labs and things where we can practice. We have had everything that I would think we need. [1N4A]

***

> We have a wide variety of opportunities in commercial certifications and training. [1B4]

***

> I think we are consistently given opportunities to go to commercial training or in-house training to keep ourselves on top of stuff. [1B4]

***

> I think it being a retrain-only career field was great because it gave us more freedom to be an adult, and not having to be around younger airmen, we have better discussions about operationally relevant stuff. And I think once you get past the fourth block, all of the information is pretty good, it's a little outdated, but the discussions are there. [1B4]

## Training Does Not Capture the "Why"

In 40 percent of our focus groups, participants talked about how training needs to include more about the overarching mission and the operational focus of their future jobs.

Participants talked about how their training often focuses on mastery of commands and rules or regulations without making connections to the goals and importance of the work that they will ultimately do. Participants talked about a need for more training and education on the "why"—with respect to both cyber training in general (i.e., across the lifespan) and IQT specifically.

> [We need training to cover] any sort of connective tissue between operations and [intelligence]. So, something that makes them operationally focused . . . to get them in an operational mindset. They can't be just writing paragraphs about cyber stuff. That's not what they are built for, and too many think that's what they are here for. I think that a lot could be solved with some sort of course that repairs that tissue or gets them in an operational mindset. [Civilian]
>
> ***
>
> The one thing that I get a complaint for every single group is, "I don't understand what I am doing. I don't know why I am doing it. I understand that I push a button, but what's that button doing? Why does the boss care?" [1N4A]
>
> ***
>
> You can understand the basics of what an IP [Internet Protocol] address is, but if you don't understand how that pertains to the target, it's irrelevant. [1N4A]
>
> ***
>
> The thing that we missed the most was the "why." We were told to point the tool from Linux at the particular thing, but the "Why would you do that? What's the theory behind it? How would you go about doing it?" were never covered. [1B4]

Participants talked about how training covers the boundaries in the field imposed by the law but not why those legal boundaries exist.

> NSA does a good job of teaching legalities—what you can't do. But not why you can't do it. So, if they're taught in their first year why they can't do some of these things, or why things are done in a certain way . . . I think that would definitely benefit them. [Civilian]

Some participants talked about how the context is important to both performance and job satisfaction.

> Make sure we are capturing the context of what we are doing. Understanding why we are doing what we are doing and that job satisfaction. . . . I do have job satisfaction because I understand the context. I understand that when I take this action . . . we did this thing and it protected this. . . . So, helping people understand that context and how they fit into the picture and how we generate airpower is important. [1B4]

## There Is a Lack of Simulations and Hands-On Practice

When discussing training issues, participants emphasized the lack of simulations and hands-on training. The concern over lack of simulations was raised in 37 percent of focus groups (Figure 3.1); in 90 percent of the discussions, simulations were suggested as something USAF could do more of to improve training. In addition, in 87 percent of the discussions, some participants talked about the need for more hands-on practice.

We also asked participants to rate how valuable certain features would be to include in training. As shown in Figure 3.3, participants felt that all of the features listed would be valuable, but they felt most strongly about the value of training against live red forces and in active simulations. Experiential learning (i.e., learning by attempting to do the work and experiencing it oneself) was also highly valued, noticeably more than over-the-shoulder learning (i.e., someone observes someone else perform the work by watching over their shoulder). We discuss the comments about simulations and live red forces first, and then we turn to the comments about hands-on and experiential learning.

### There Is a Lack of Simulations, Training Ranges, Live Red Forces, and Capture the Flag

Participants, particularly in 1B4 focus groups, were concerned about the lack of simulations in initial training. They articulated that there are currently not enough simulations or quality training ranges and emphasized the important role of simulations during initial training and as individuals begin their first assignments in cyber.

> I don't think we have enough [simulations and hands-on training]. Like when learning to hunt. [Training is] still death by PowerPoint. It's still "watch videos." And they expect them to do these missions based on watching a video. [1B4]

> ***

> We absolutely need access to a good training range. I'm the newest of the three of us here; I've had maybe two days of actually doing a mission. That is the only time I've had to actually practice tools and actually learn to build upon my skills. I went to training, I got certification, it took me two months to get to the point where I could even test my skills because that training range is not available to me on a daily basis and our personnel can't test their skills, learn new skills, learn how to properly use the software without that test range. The only time our people get to test those skills is on mission, and that is not the time to learn how to use something. [1B4]

> ***

> If the Air Force could invest in anything that would either [build up the] course or experience after the course, it would be a centralized and well-thought-out and built-out training range that would allow access to a full range of technical challenges. . . . It would be a set of systems that would allow people to practice operations in a contained classroom environment. [1B4]

31

Concerns about the lack of simulations also arose in discussions of continuation training. Participants are concerned that, because they do not have access to simulations during continuation training, it is more difficult to keep their skills relevant, and their only hands-on practice is during live missions.

> As we have built cyber, we have not built out training and framework. We don't have sims for weapon systems or ranges so we can train folks. We have some, but not for all weapon systems. That is problematic because the training they do is on the live network, which is not ideal. [Workforce—other[33]]

***

> So, [some cyber personnel] can sit down and get on the keyboard . . . just play on this network and figure out how to do this technique and continue to keep your skills from atrophying. We don't have that. [Workforce—other]

Participants explained that, although practice ranges might exist, they are not accessible on all bases or to all personnel who need them, and greater demand than supply of existing ranges makes it difficult to access these resources.

> We could use a virtual range, and I don't think we have one here at Scott. It'd be vital. I went to a training at Carnegie Mellon, and it was great. [1N4A]

***

> In Hawaii, we had our own range, and it was pretty good. We had time for hands-on keyboard, and, six months later, we went on a live mission, and I felt a lot more ready than if I hadn't had it. [1N4A]

***

> There are a lot of ranges. When we request, they say they cannot support us. Accessibility is an issue. There are ranges, and there are environments, but we cannot get to them. [Civilian]

In addition to reports of too few opportunities for simulations and the existence of too few virtual ranges, participants discussed the challenges associated with the limited quality and capacity of existing USAF simulation resources. Some participants also mentioned ranges that were paid for but never delivered.

> One of the biggest things that people need is a training range where you can build virtual networks inside of and then practice your training inside of this environment. . . . Our group has a contract with a company to maintain and build our training ranges. We've had the contract for a year now and have only gotten one range the entire time that is shared with every unit in the group and we have to allot time in. Nobody ever gets to use this thing, and getting access to these individuals [contractor] to be able to set up, add time to this range, is almost impossible. [1B4]

***

---

[33] *Other* encompasses anyone not in the 1B4, 1N4A, or civilian category.

I think we have a capacity issue in terms of licenses. We have four squadrons in SA [San Antonio] using the same sim space. Within four months, they have used up all of the licenses. We need enough scenarios for the ranges and need at a minimum 24-hour notice. [1B4]

\*\*\*

There is a range for the Title 10 side, but it is not very well maintained. It is kind of confusing how you get time on that range, and it takes longer to get time on the range than you actually have to practice. There is not a huge availability on the Title 10 side. [1B4]

Participants also talked about why more ranges and better access to ranges are needed and the benefits that might be accrued. (As shown in Figure 3.2, this was offered as a suggested training change or solution in 90 percent of the discussions.)

We need a training range, a place to simulate activities with good support to spin up what we need. We need to replicate live traffic, malicious activity, and the ability to go beyond the normal network, and we need the ability to have access to that infrastructure. Currently, we do not have access to any of the simulation spaces or ranges, and there's not enough hosts to go around to support multiple groups. [1B4]

\*\*\*

Having more of a realistic mockup . . . where these aren't clean boxes and we are going in and we are the only person on that box, because we never run into that in the real world. Having more realistic simulations where they could have simulated active users or not such a clean box or network. [1B4]

\*\*\*

Definitely more active [simulations], as much realistic training as possible. Practice like you are going to play, especially in the OCO world. I mean, you are going against people who are constantly attacking you, and you have to be able to react as soon as possible, but yet we train to sit at a computer. Reaction time is key. How fast can someone enter our network? We are trained to take our time and bounce off a few people; we are not trained to think and how to react. [This is] important in the OCO and DCO world. Someone attacks your network, how to defend? You cannot take all day. . . . [M]ore and more they will be in your network no matter how many firewalls you have up. You have to figure out how to defend it. [1N4A]

\*\*\*

Having [ranges] for newcomers to the unit who may not have all of their access yet, and can't actually start to learn the mission, but they can learn something—generic cyber skills. And then also have another training network for those on missions, that we specifically own and use, and can be tailored to the needs of that mission set, would also be beneficial. [1B4]

One participant also explained that simulations may boost morale, allow for assessment of skills, and offer opportunities for mentorship and development of junior personnel by more-senior personnel.

A lot of these folks that work in this environment also really just enjoy getting on [simulations]. People that are really good at it want to get on, they want to do capture the flag, they do these things for fun on their own time. If we could offer up . . . part of their duty day to sit down and do a little capture-the-flag time every so often where we can measure their performance and some of these more seniors help the juniors through. To do that could do a couple of things. It could keep skills relevant, keep skills from atrophying. It could help with job satisfaction because, every once in a while, you get to go sit down and have some fun and go free wherever they want. That's where tactical exercises come into play. . . . If I swing the bat at someone throwing me practice pitches, it gets me closer to being ready for when the fast ball and the curve ball [are thrown]. That's one thing that we don't have enough of in cyber. [Workforce—other]

A number of participants cautioned that both live red forces and training ranges might be useful in some circumstances but not in others. (This view is reflected in the opposite sentiment expressed in 13 percent of discussions shown in Figure 3.2.) In particular, participants pointed to the benefits of simple simulations or ranges for training and practicing specific skill sets. However, they noted that it is much more difficult to design simulations that are more complex and replicate reality. They also explained that such complex ranges and simulations would need to be constantly updated to maintain currency as cyber evolves. With this in mind, some suggested that, to design valuable training ranges, there would need to be airmen whose sole job is dedicated to doing so. Those participants suggested dedicating a squadron to building ranges, servers, networks, and other resources. This was in line with a similar recommendation to have a unit dedicated to maintaining training equipment (e.g., computers with proper software installed).

Some participants explained that having airmen fill dedicated roles to develop training resources would be preferable to the current practice of pulling individuals away from mission-related work to develop training. Moreover, participants said that in-house individuals would be best equipped to track ongoing threats and technological developments and design and integrate mission-relevant training scenarios.

Some did not agree with the idea of creating dedicated positions using civilian or military personnel.[34] In some cases, participants said that private-sector ranges might be superior to any developed in house, specifically because the private-sector personnel specialize in designing them. Lastly, a few noted that NSA-developed ranges and others used by joint entities might be shareable, and some elements of them could possibly be given to USAF to build from. Participants described this as an opportunity to avoid reinventing the wheel and even noted that sharing such simulation technology across the services might help save resources.

---

[34] We did not code for this specific comment, so it is not reflected with counts in the figures, but it did come up in some instances when participants were brainstorming about the best ways to generate additional simulations and to avoid some of the potential pitfalls of attempting to build ranges without the appropriate resources and expertise.

## *Hands-On and Experiential Learning Are Beneficial*

Participants described a variety of benefits of hands-on learning: it improves knowledge retention, better prepares operators to work in real missions, helps identify areas of improvement, and can work well being integrated with over-the-shoulder learning. Some of the comments describing the improvement of knowledge retention are as follows:

> I think we definitely need to be on keyboard. Over-the-shoulder [learning] goes so far, but you don't remember it. Like anything else, you build the muscle memory. . . . Maybe one time watching somebody do it, but then we need to be on keyboard. [1B4]

> \*\*\*

> OJT [on-the-job] training and hands-on [learning] is how you really remember in this field. You can read or look up on your own what information is, but doing it is an entirely different story. [1N4A]

> \*\*\*

> I think putting someone to a job and letting them learn how to do it by doing it. Having someone [explain], "This is how you do this," without them actually doing it until way later, after you've taught them, then they could lose that [information] without learning it. Definitely letting them do it instead of watching someone do it is what I'd recommend. [1N4A]

Participants also noted that experiential learning was best for teaching operators about working in a mission, where they would need skills that would not necessarily be taught in a book or in a lecture.

> I would encourage tactical training and exercise to work those muscles. I say this from an Air Force perspective. When we have bombers and fighters, those pilots are expected to run regular sorties to stay mission capable. We don't view the cyber domain in the same way. . . . But if you actually go and observe the operation, it looks very similar; there is a hand on the button to push the bombs, there is a pilot that is running the entire thing, and there is a navigator that is running through the operation. It is very similar, but we don't have a proficiency requirement to run regular training to keep our folks proficient on how the mission is actually run. The Air Force does it very well with airplanes; we haven't viewed cyber as being the same kind of domain as air, and we really need to change our perspective in that manner. There is no avenue right now to do that kind of tactical exercise on a regular basis on a regular rotation for our 1N4As and 1N4Bs. [1N4A]

> \*\*\*

> A lot of the time, you are planning or doing research, but if you do not utilize skills, you lose them. During cyber exercises, they are taking their skills and putting them to work. This is making them better analysts. Before getting to the real world, you can learn from mistakes and not make them when you get to real-world actions. [1N4A]

Others explained that a benefit of hands-on training was that it gave operators an opportunity to identify areas in which they could improve and possibly even identify continuation training to help overcome their shortcomings.

> The biggest thing I liked about UCT [undergraduate cyber training, the colloquial term for Cyber Warfare Operations—Apprentice Course] was block 6 when we just had time. They just gave us lab time, and the instructor would come in for questions, but, for the most part, it was just us at terminals playing around. That's where the real learning happens. That's what I liked about UCT, more so than other training I've had. A lot of time you don't have the time to just be working on a range, make mistakes, and figure out the process for yourself. The time to just be on keyboard and play was really valuable to me. [1B4]

***

> You can go to all of the training—all the SANS, Route 9B [a company that provides commercial training], CNOQC [Computer Network Operations Qualification Course]—it's all good training, but nothing compares to actual on keyboard on mission. Get on mission; start doing things. If you have a technical deficiency or a training gap, then you should be able to almost on demand go to training—if you identify on mission that you don't know an area as well as you should, they should have the flexibility to immediately put you on training and to do that remotely. [1B4]

***

> Just having the flexibility to get on mission and start to actually do things on keyboard. Then, when you identify that someone isn't as strong as they need to be in something, then have people self-identify that they need help in an area and take initiative to go out and learn what they need. [1B4]

When participants were asked whether they preferred experiential or over-the-shoulder learning, many stated that a combination of both was most beneficial. Some noted that observing others would help as an introduction to a topic, and others believed that having both was necessary to account for operators with different learning styles.

> If stakes are high, you will absolutely need that person over your shoulder, but really, you want a combination of both, depending on how people learn best. Your model should be able to adapt to that. I like both of the models. There comes a point when a person becomes autonomous, but they need the ability to continue to further their knowledge—if that is what they desire, and the organization requires that. Autonomy is the goal. Once you become autonomous, it is your job to start training and mentoring other people as well. [1N4A]

***

> Over the shoulder is good, but experiential is better. Over the shoulder is like, if you make a mistake, they will say, "OK, try this and try that." But experience, if something didn't work, it gets you to think outside the box to get to the solution without the extra help. [1N4A]

***

Both; sometimes I need to watch people who are better than me to observe them and learn. We also need a safe place to try it and a safe place to fail. Currently, they're both working well, but I can't control the over-the-shoulder thing, because that's a personal preference, and, for situations where people can fail, I don't control that, because it's somewhere else. [1B4]

## Current Instructional Methods Are Ineffective

In 33 percent of focus groups, participants talked about ineffective instructional methods in their training courses. Participants' comments centered on teaching strategy and curricular structure. Participants questioned the pedagogy, operational experience, and investment of instructors. They also explained that the structure was suboptimal for the acquisition and later application of skills and knowledge necessary for the 1B4 and 1N4A career fields. Concerns about instructional methods were not limited to initial training; they also arose with regard to continuation training.

When discussing teaching strategy, participants articulated concerns about the model of instruction. In a conversation with leadership, a participant expressed the view that the "old-school" stand-and-deliver model was not an effective way to develop operational proficiency.

> We learned in Keesler [that] training was way too old-school. You sit in class for three weeks to go through a module and then are being told to go do it. [Workforce—other]

1B4s and 1N4As also shared concerns about instruction. Many comments centered on concerns about pedagogy because of the concentration of content, testing intervals, and inadequate responses to questions.

> I don't think giving all material you'd learn in a semester of college and testing the next day is good. And if you ask questions, they say to read it in the book. A lot of instructors will be teaching, and someone asks an advanced question, and they deflect and move on because they don't know the answer. [1B4]

A similar concern was raised in a number of focus groups. Participants shared the belief that the current models of instruction and assessment are not oriented toward true learning and identification of aptitude. They articulated concerns that this "fire hose" method does not do an effective job of training or identifying talent.

> RIOT [Remote Interactive Operator Training] is not about training. It's about finding people who can do the job and just have enough luck to not fail in the first 30 days. [1B4]

> \*\*\*

> What you get in UCT is not really training. They bombard you with tests. Then, we go to CWO, which is good because, there, they want to teach and aren't just there to weed you out. I walked out of CWO thinking I really learned something. [1B4]

> \*\*\*

Unfortunately, since we have to get them something quickly, they get material one day and test the next. They cram material. Sometimes, the material is poorly written. Doing PowerPoint to death is not training people. Sometimes, for cyber, it's better to do hands-on. We don't do enough of that. I think when you spend four months of cramming new topics into your mind and are expected to retain it until you get to a new command. [1B4]

***

They push so much information so fast that the majority of operators can't retain it by the time they get to the unit. [1B4]

***

The training I experienced was a very traditional military training environment. It [IST] was fire hose; you are presented with tons of information, the stuff that is really important and you will hear more than once. But I wouldn't say that we are dropping the ball on preparing. [1N4A]

A number of participants questioned whether instructors were invested in their development. One participant connected this perceived lack of interest in the work and its outcomes to the fact that instructor positions are filled by mandated assignment, and many instructors lack operational experience.

[My instructors were] not very good. They were intelligent, and 30 percent of them were positive. But many were disgruntled, and some didn't have real-world experience. Some were mandated to be teachers rather than wanting to do it themselves. One had to teach the networking block but didn't have a networking background. If you're trying to teach people, you have to want to do it. [1B4]

Participants also raised concerns about instruction in external courses. They reported that contractors hired to provide continuation training are ineffective instructors.

The ones taught by Hurlburt and Keesler were well designed. It's when they go in the field and get the contractors that the problem would occur. They would teach from the slides and just read from them, and it wasn't the same as real teaching and learning. [Civilian]

***

Most training revolves around certs [certifications], so, if you get these certs, you're trained. But the companies in charge of these certs aren't really training you; they're just training you how to get the certs. They'll say, "The test will probably ask you questions about this." So, they'll teach you how to do that, but not how to apply it in a practical setting. [1N4A]

Not all of the participants shared negative perceptions of the instruction. Some shared appreciation for the teaching strategy and experience of their instructors (see the opposite sentiment offered by 13 percent in Figure 3.1).

Given the material they had to present, they presented very well. They were seasoned—they had a lot of experience. What they could tell us, they got me excited salivating from the stories they told. Some came from OCO, some DCO. Some were better than others; [with some] you are just looking at firewall all

38

day. Some came from the squadron that I was in, and that got me excited because I found out that I got to travel. [1B4]

As they discussed the shortcomings of current instructional practice, participants shared their perspectives on how instructional quality could be improved. Their recommendations included selection of instructors with more operational experience (see Figures 3.2 and 3.3).

In one discussion, it was suggested that USAF could learn from current trends in higher education and implement a technology-driven, flipped curriculum. Such instructional practice would make learning more applied because students would work on foundational material independently with instructors, in more of a shoulder-to-shoulder tutoring role, as needed. In this model, direct instruction could be limited to brief discussions of more-advanced material before applied exercises.

> Some of the recommendations that were made—take the delivery of course content and make it more self-paced and challenge based. This is similar to what we see in a college setting, where a lot of cyber curriculum is going into an inverted style of teaching where students learn from hands-on labs and the teacher becomes more of a mentor than a lecturer. . . . They learn better by doing and having to struggle, not by memorizing. [Workforce—other]

Some participants also talked about how USAF's traditional 3-, 5-, 7-, and 9-level approach to training might not necessarily fit well for the cyber workforce. They explained that, because cyber is a rapidly changing field, skills can atrophy or become quickly outdated. As a result, it would not be unreasonable for some 3-levels to be much more current or adept in certain specialized areas than 5-, 7- or 9-levels. Given this, a linear approach to training might not be sensible.

Some participants suggested that instruction may have improved over time as USAF has placed instructors with greater experience in the schoolhouse. Such comments suggest the perception that direct experience increases instructional quality.

> I think it's getting better now because the Air Force is getting people who have actually experienced the field. I became an OCO instructor, and other operators I have worked with went on to the schoolhouse. I think quality of instructors is really important in teaching the new folks. [1B4]

Not all participants put a premium on operational experience. For example, one participant articulated an appreciation for quality instructional methods and a belief that instructional efficacy can be independent of field experience.

> I recall having an instructor in my IQT whose job prior was in construction. He had no real experience in the field itself. He was just teaching from his material, and he was probably the best instructor that I had. If someone has something to teach and they are able to teach, then I don't think it is important. Now, he couldn't really relate the material to the real world, so that lacked. But it depends on the subject. If it is just knowledge based, experience is not needed. Being able to teach someone is the most important thing. But, if we are talking about something that is very technical, then it would be beneficial. [1N4A]

Participants also offered several related suggestions for how best to address these issues. These suggestions are discussed in the following sections.

## Training Should Be Targeted to the Specialized Skill Sets Needed for Each Mission

Participants in more than half of discussions expressed the need to provide the workforce with specialized training to match their skill sets and missions. Participants expressed the view that USAF should define specific work roles and tailor training to support those work roles. Participants from the 1B4, 1N4A, and civilian workforces shared this sentiment.

> We need to provide just-in-time training. We need to say, "Here is your mission, here's what you need to learn to do that," and have those resources available for them. [1B4]

***

> We are tiptoeing around the skill set by providing anything around cyber to try to improve airmen's jobs, but it's not [working]. [Training] needs to be work-role specific. Many other career fields have specific job training that enables them to do their job. Because people see cyber as so new, they want us to learn everything. It's not possible during a two-week course a couple times a year. You can't be an expert like that. What I've seen in the past that's successful is ops [operations]-specific training—in-house training that taught them how to do the job exactly. [1N4A]

***

> There is so much in the field as a whole, so you can't touch everything. If we had better definition of the work roles that we will be fulfilling, gearing the training more towards those work roles will help. Not saying what is current isn't beneficial; it is just that tailoring a bit more . . . [to what] we will do most likely. [1N4A]

Others added that cyber technology and tactics change rapidly. To match the ever-changing nature of the job, airmen should be allowed to focus on specific skills and continue to receive additional training on those skills to stay current. One leader explained,

> Cyber tech changes so rapidly; the tactics, environments change. How do you keep your people current? I had trouble with my master sergeants [knowing] less about the tech than my brand-new airmen [because the new airmen] had more-recent training. . . . So, if they update a technology, who needs that? . . . How do I deliver that to those who need it? Those are the challenges. That's the model I would go to. You chunk them into smaller pieces of discrete technologies. You then provide them in a way folks can get to at any point in their career. . . . Right now, it doesn't support that. We need that. [Workforce—other]

## Offensive Cyber Operations and Defensive Cyber Operations Should Be Taught to Everyone

In 27 percent of focus groups, participants shared the opinion that OCO and DCO skill sets should be taught to all recruits. Participants articulated the view that work in an offensive or defensive capacity would be improved by a greater knowledge about the other side.

> I think they should be trained on both, because I think that gives you a better background. If you do DCO and you have the OCO training, you will have a better defender. [1N4A]

***

> I don't think [training] needs to be improved; I think it needs to be shared more. They are dividing DCO and OCO, and I think all 1B4[s] should have knowledge of both right out of tech [school]. [1B4]

During discussions of comprehensive OCO and DCO training, some participants spoke broadly of standardization of training across sites and roles.

> Looking at training, it should be standardized. Whether I'm stationed here or wherever. The training for my work roles should be standardized. I should get [the] same training to do those functions at whatever base it is. Until we can codify what those work roles are, it's tough to do. We need to codify what those work roles are. [Workforce—other]

Advocates made the point that there are not stark distinctions between OCO and DCO roles.

> I wouldn't say that a split would be beneficial. I have worked sig [signals intelligence on the] development side for five years, and then I switched to operations, and having that [signals intelligence] background really amplified my ability to be an EA [exploitation analyst][35] because there is a lot of overlap. [1N4A]

***

> A lot of analytical work that needs to be done, as well as operations. I would never want to draw a line between anything. Everything builds off of each other, despite vast differences. [1N4A]

Accordingly, participants expressed that the major differences in OCO and DCO training are not appropriate given the functions and missions that these individuals fulfill. One 1B4 conveyed that differences in the depth and rigor of OCO and DCO training could be remedied by a comprehensive model. This individual maintained that, at present, OCO training develops a better technical skill set that would also be advantageous in DCOs.

> I personally feel that all operators need that level of training. There should not be a difference in what one operator does; in the end of [the] day, we are all assets, and we should be interchangeable [with] each other. It shouldn't be OCO or DCO. I should be able to flip my hat at any given time and go do offensive

---

[35] Exploitation analysts are one type of cyber professional. For more information, see Montes, 2017.

action. I understand why they separate it, but, from a learning perspective, everyone needs to be trained the exact same so we can communicate on the same level. There is a different level of education between OCO and DCO. You can tell there is a difference when you communicate with them on a technical level. You can tell they had very focused training, and they can speak on the technology. DCO don't have that depth of knowledge. [1B4]

In one discussion, a participant identified that combining OCO and DCO training might be best suited to continuation training for particular roles, specifically leadership and reverse engineers:[36]

But if I am building someone to be a reverse engineer, both OCO and DCO, then their training may be the exact same. . . . You see differentiation, but much more at the technical space, not leadership. I don't mean that in a rank way, as you start talking about grooming and know how to make risk decisions, I think that is where the training begins to overlap a lot more. Those who are leading attack and those who are leading defense squadrons on the officer side, their training should probably be exactly the same. But if they are on the keyboard operating, then there is some differentiation for sure. [Workforce—other]

Some participants pushed back during these discussions, advocating to keep OCO and DCO training separate. One participant said that the status quo better tailors training to particular jobs.

Having [training] more relatable to the actual job because CWO [IQT] was a combination of a whole bunch of different kinds of people, offensive and defensive. Having more tailored to what you are going to actually do. Having an offensive one and a defensive one. [1B4]

---

[36] Reverse engineering is one approach used in cyber work and an area in which some cyber operators specialize.

# 4. Timely Access to Training and the Currency of Training Resources

This chapter elaborates on the comments relating to two broad topic areas raised by participants: issues with the timing of and access to needed training and issues with resources not keeping pace with cyber. Figure 4.1 contains the issues that were raised by participants in more than three focus groups, and Figure 4.2 lists the related solutions that were suggested by participants in more than three groups. We discuss each of the issues individually in the sections that follow.

**Figure 4.1. What Needs to Be Improved in Training: Timing, Access, and Resources**

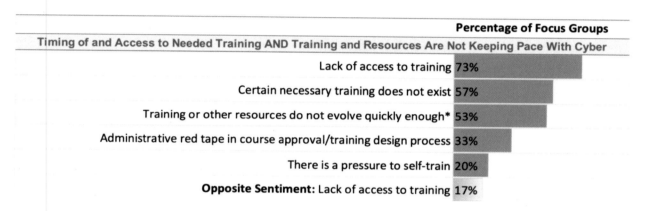

NOTE: For some topics, no opposite sentiment was expressed in the workforce discussions. Where an opposite sentiment was expressed in 3 to 7 percent of the workforce focus groups (i.e., one or two groups), the category is marked with an asterisk. Percentages represent the number of focus groups in which a topic was mentioned by at least one person. All percentages are out of a total of 30 discussions.

**Figure 4.2. Satisfaction with Training Opportunities**

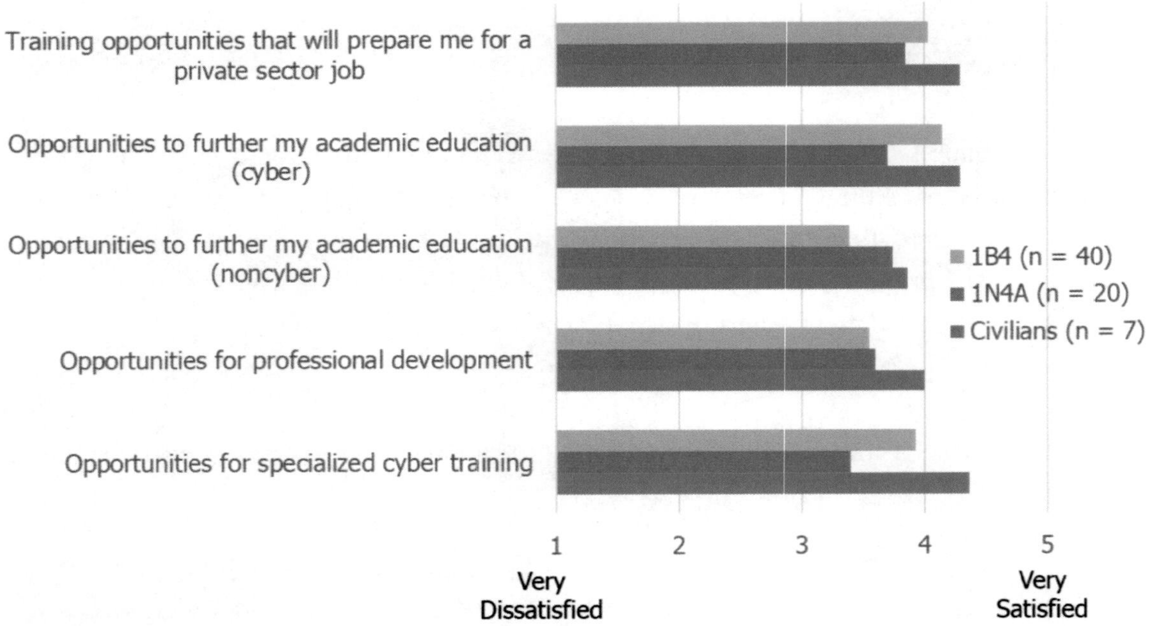

## Timing of and Access to Needed Training Present Challenges

### There Is Lack of Access to Existing Training

Across focus groups, participants articulated a variety of frustrations related to access to training. It was widely held that, in many cases, the training exists but individuals face challenges in gaining access to participate. Interestingly, this runs counter to participants' questionnaire responses to items about satisfaction with training opportunities (shown in Figure 4.2).[37] In one discussion, a participant put it simply: "Everything we need access to exists. Getting access is an issue."

When participants described why there are issues with training access, they cited capacity issues related to time, funding for courses, seats in courses, and existence and capacity of training ranges. Participants' time-related access concerns focused on the infeasibility of getting specialized training designed quickly enough to gain experience before a mission.

One participant expressed the view that each mission requires a tailored practice environment, which is currently impossible to develop in a timely fashion.

> The problem is that every mission is different within the same terrain. Most of the time, we need something very specialized in the training range. . . . It comes

---

[37] As a reminder, the questionnaire was administered prior to the focus group discussions so that questionnaire responses were not influenced by the comments raised during the discussions.

44

down to a mission. We go out and say we need a range before we can execute in a month, and they say that we cannot get it done in a month. [Civilian]

Participants also talked about the amount of time that it takes to procure new equipment and materials; this timeline delays training and development.

For us, unfortunately, we have all the funds we need for equipment, [but there are] some issues with the procurement process. It can take six months to a year to acquire. And the cyber picture may have changed [by then]. The time delay that it takes to get [equipment] exceeds the time to work those same things. [Workforce—other]

Some participants talked about a perennial lack of resources for continuation training in general. Others talked about how funding on a fiscal year cycle means that there might not be money when it is needed.

So, then we project that out and get everyone signed up for—spend, spend, spend, spend—and then you get toward the end of the year and . . . we don't have the funds anymore. [1B4]

\*\*\*

We have tons of money for operations, and not enough for training. When we need money from training, we're told that we don't have money because all our money is for operations. [1B4]

\*\*\*

The reserves don't really pay for training; the active-duty guys will go to vendor training and will get specialized training, but they do not want to pay for reservists. [1B4]

\*\*\*

[Civilians] need the range, and we need to be in the training rooms to work. But we don't have the resources. We can practice on our own at home, but that is not the same as being on the network: retrieving logs, knowing how to bypass things in the system. We need continuation training by means of workshops. We need the training that SANS [Institute] provides. SANS training is provided but not practically applied. For us, everyone shares that feeling. We need to be working on it. [Civilian]

Some participants talked about delays and a lack of seats in courses.

The CWO course is really haphazard on whether I can send my guys, because we have to fight for seats. [1B4]

\*\*\*

It took me four tries to get into retraining—I kept getting denied. . . . They would approve me and then deny me if they approved too many people by accident. Another time, I was denied because of budget cuts. [1B4]

\*\*\*

There is a lot of opportunity. It's just that not everyone gets to attend these trainings, and that is the downfall. Our host agencies and stuff like that have these courses, but the demand for training is so heavy that people are waiting months to years to get certain trainings done. The availability hurts, but the opportunity is there. [1N4A]

\*\*\*

A lot of people want to do [Cyber 200] training, but I will have to wait at least another year depending on whether or not I make rank. [1N4A]

\*\*\*

They always take the officers and enlisted first, then comes us. [Civilian]

\*\*\*

I'm pretty much sitting around burning the clock until I can get into the next training. . . . I failed out of CNOQC, and now I'm waiting around doing admin work until I can access [the next course]. After three-plus years of training, go, go, go, and then—psh. [1B4]

Some participants noted that the issue is partly caused by the joint nature of the work and the fact that USAF is reliant on the availability of courses that are provided by agencies outside USAF, and seats are shared with the other services. Some participants also explained that, even in joint assignments, access to training can vary drastically.

For my four years, I was in cyber command and I took less classes than I took in six months working in an NSA billet. There needs to be more opportunities for people in cyber command—it's pretty bleak. [1N4A]

This issue of availability of joint training does come up in other USAF communities (e.g., special operations), where it can also create training bottlenecks. To the extent that this issue is occurring in multiple high-skill career fields (e.g., cyber, special operations), USAF might benefit from a broader look at it and its potential impacts on the workforce's skills and overall readiness.

One participant talked about being unable to take a course again even though it is now more relevant than it was previously: "It's crazy that we are willing to spend $6,000 a pop on SANS courses but we won't send people back through IQT that has been revamped and that is actually tailored to our weapons systems" [1B4].

Some participants pointed out that the geographic distribution of courses and seats might not map to the need.

So, [each course is] only offered in certain places. I know they tried to get me into [a course] in Hawaii. So, that's a TDY [temporary duty] that the squadron would have to pay for that it's very unlikely they'll pay for. But it's the only one offered in a year. [1N4A]

\*\*\*

I see classes that are offered anywhere but Maryland, and they always have seats. But there's no way I can get there. [1N4A]

Lack of training ranges and capacity in training ranges were also mentioned. (See Chapter 3 for more on this topic.)

On a positive note, 17 percent of participants expressed the opposite sentiment about the availability of and access to training (see Figure 4.1). Some participants articulated the view that, in some cases, they had witnessed persistent self-advocacy lead to better access to training. Other individuals expressed that they have sufficient funding for and access to training.

> This is the first unit I have been in that has the funds for training. But in previous units, you really had to fight tooth and nail to get continuous training. When they don't provide that, it is up to the individual to keep themselves proficient. [1B4]

***

> I am current[ly] enrolled in [course name], but, to get to that point, I really had to push leadership to approve the training even though it falls right in line with my [position]. [1B4]

***

> I think a lot of our training gaps are already addressed at the unit level. We have really good funding for TDY and training in general. I think people have a lot of opportunities to get that third-party training they need and learn things they haven't encountered yet. . . . I think our unit is a little different. I think we get significantly more training money than most. [1B4]

***

> I'm afforded quite a bit of opportunities. They asked what courses you would be interested in doing. We can send those up, and, most of the time, it gets approved and I'm able to go to those courses. [1B4]

***

> I've not heard of many people getting taken out of training due to funding, [or] even [being] denied training that they've requested. [Civilian]

Although participants occasionally articulated the view that their particular career field is related to the inaccessibility of training, we did not notice any qualitative differences in reports of access to training among 1B4s, 1N4As, and civilians.[38]

> 1N4As are given JCAC and then never talked to again. . . . We don't have the regular rinse-and-repeat training that happens [for other career fields]. [1N4A]

Some participants who had experienced multiple assignments were able to describe the ways in which access to training varies by assignment (e.g., related to squadron resources, geographic demand for seats in a course, staffed in an NSA assignment).

> I've never been in a unit that would turn you down for a [certificate] as long as you justify it. [1N4A]

---

[38] By *qualitative differences*, we mean that the nature of their comments seemed similar. That is, regardless of whether the counts of the comments were the same, the descriptive content of the comments could be substantively different. But in this case, we did not hear anything that would lead us to conclude that the comments were substantively different. If we had noted such differences, we would have coded them separately. Sample sizes are too small to detect statistically significant differences in the counts of these types of comments.

***

Coming from Cyber Command, there were so many classes and [opportunities] out there from the NSA. Cyber Command could not get into that. I had to wait for open seats to get in. There needs to be more opportunities for people in Cyber Command—it's pretty bleak. [1N4A]

***

I have been sent to a squad that does not support cyber. . . . As a result, I have lost a lot of cyber training opportunities. I have talked to people from other sister units who say they have had training opportunities to go to DEFCON [defense readiness condition], [but] they won't set aside any funding for us. It can depend on what unit you land [in] and how much that unit is willing to dedicate. It [can] also pigeonhole [you] to a work role as an EA. I have wanted to go through JCAC or RIOT, but, because of the unit I landed in, they don't have billets for me to expand on. [1N4A]

***

[The opportunity for training] massively exists here from the agency side. If we went down to Texas, I bet it exists a whole lot less. [1N4A]

Participants repeatedly mentioned how it can be difficult to access NSA training. However, this issue is not under USAF's control.

When I mentioned getting into classes, that's pretty much all NSA and not Air Force. . . . There are NSA shops that have private classes. If you're not in that shop, then they'll tell you that you can't take it because it's a reserved class, but there are open seats. [1N4A]

***

[NSA] does not give Air Force any priority with classes that are mandatory for us to take for our job roles. If an NSA person needs it, the NSA person gets priority. So, what he's saying where it could take [a] year and a half to get into [the] course because he has six requirements that they're not even letting him into because he's Air Force personnel. [1N4A]

***

The Air Force relies on [NSA]-specific classes for its training pipelines. That creates a dependency on the agency that we don't have any control over. We come to them as a customer for certain classes. We are mandated for a CYBERCOM unit to have these NSA classes, but we may not be able to get into those same classes even though it's a requirement per the work role. We need to look at the actual certification pipelines and remove agency-specific requirements and find alternatives to those to where we are not reliant solely on the agency for certifications. [1N4A]

Although such NSA training might be difficult for some to access, a 1N4A SME explained that some airmen might not realize that they are still receiving some of the best training available to the cyber workforce.

> It is difficult for those on Title 10 billets colocated at an NSA site to be given access to NSA training. Our airmen assigned to NSA have some of the best training that can be offered. [SME]

Overall, participants reported that they have limited access to continuation training and that squadrons are thus left to do their best to find or produce opportunities to develop their own. One participant said, "Training has been pushed to the side, and whatever you can figure out and bring to the table yourself is what you are using."

Participants underscored that the current level of access to training is unacceptable given the importance of their mission. One participant put the bottom line simply: "When you need training, you should be able to go to training."

### Certain Necessary Training Does Not Exist

When asked about gaps in training and resources, participants described the nonexistence of or limited variety in training. With regard to initial training, participants spoke about particular skill sets and foundational content that are missing at present. The bulk of the discussion centered on the nonexistence of or paltry options for continuation training. It was clear from discussions within and across focus groups that there were differences in knowledge of and access to continuation training.

> We are given very little continuous training after we leave tech school. We get some commercial [training] if someone can find it. Or, when a mission comes up around one topic, we try to scrape together a training for one thing. But it is not continuous. It is, "get as much information as you can," or "try to figure out what you can figure out." [1B4]

***

> We don't have much continuation training. It is a lot of outside organizations for training or the different agencies—that is really the continuation training we receive. There really isn't another level of training like a regular schoolhouse. There is one course you can take that is about six weeks long, but it is not as technical. It is more concepts and planning; it is not a technical continuation. [Technical continuation training] doesn't really exist for the Air Force. Intermediate to expert [technical continuation training] would help a lot. [1N4A]

1B4s tended to mention a lack of training altogether, whereas 1N4As articulated gaps in the availability of particular kinds of training. There were limited comments from civilians regarding a lack of training, but, because of the small number of civilian focus group participants, this might not be representative of the overall civilian cyber workforce.

Participants also pointed to specific training that exists in certain places but is not accessible to all. For example, someone mentioned that a RIOT prep course developed by the 315th Training Squadron in Texas is not accessible to everyone. Someone else mentioned that it would be helpful to have designated training for developers; if an individual gets assigned to a developer squadron, then that person goes to developer training, which might be what is currently done in the 90th Cyberspace Operations Squadron. One participant explained that continuation training in cyber should be thought about in a way that was similar to the pilot model for maintaining currency.

> When we have bombers and fighters, those pilots are expected to run regular sorties to stay mission capable. . . . We don't view the cyber domain in the same way. But if you actually go and observe the operation, it looks very similar. . . . but we don't have a proficiency requirement to run regular training to keep our folks proficient on how the mission is actually ran. The Air Force does it very well with airplanes. We haven't viewed cyber as being the same kind of domain as air, and we really need to change our perspective in that manner. There is no avenue right now to do that kind of tactical exercise on a regular basis on a regular rotation for our 1N4As and 1N4Bs. [1N4A]

Continuation training that does exist is often inapplicable to the assignment.

> Most deficiencies I can identify seem to stem from the Air Force's inability to adapt to having personnel in the [National Security] Agency. A lot of these roles, when we talk about upgrade training, classes through the Air Force . . . . They just aren't applicable or realistically available to us as things presently stand. [1N4A]

Other participants suggested that the amount of continuation training varies by cyber assignment.

> This is my third assignment in our career field. My first assignment, I had zero continuation training. We were at the maintenance squadron. In general, they did not facilitate any continuation training . . . for us while we were there. From there, I jumped to a joint NSA–Air Force assignment, and I went through the [RIOT] pipeline. That pipeline was seven months—it's actually built very well for continuation training. . . . Then, coming here, the training really wasn't too much of a continuation training as it was a, "Hey, this is how you turn on the device" [type of training]. [1B4]
>
> ***
>
> I'm not entirely certain what [continuation training CYBERCOM runs], but they don't do training for analysts. They spend a lot of time on training for operators, but they don't do that for analysts, and that's what the 1N4As are primarily doing. [1N4A]
>
> ***
>
> It depends on the site. [Where I used to work], we spent a lot of time on the analysts. [1N4A]

### There Is Pressure to Self-Train

Participants noted that the training currently offered to them does not adequately meet the knowledge and skill development that cyber demands. Airmen feel that they must supplement official training with off-duty training, such as by taking college courses or self-training at home.

> I need to get extra coursework from college to keep my skill level and be the analyst that I am. I do that on my own time. I think it would set you apart, it makes you a better analyst. Since it is not required, a lot of people will not do it,

and I think it hurts the mission a bit. It sucks that you have to, though. It's a lot. [1N4A]

***

We were told that we need to practice this stuff at home if we want to be good. I have three kids. [1B4]

It is worth noting that this pressure to self-train does come up in other career fields, but it might be exacerbated in the cyber field and especially relevant to it because of the constantly changing nature of the field.

## Training and Resources Are Not Keeping Pace with Cyber

### Training and Other Resources Do Not Evolve Quickly Enough

As the landscape of cybersecurity advances, operators need to be up to date with the latest technology and techniques. In roughly half of the discussions, participants indicated that the resources and trainings are not updated enough. As a result, cyber operators are either unprepared or unable to keep pace to maintain currency. The participants indicated that the lack of updates is a result of either bureaucratic issues or insufficient resources, such as money or equipment. The following are examples of comments about insufficient resources:

A lot of the skills and technologies change regularly, so, unlike a linguist, our targets that we are trying to learn about are changing technology, and we have to be on top of all of that. We are expected to stay on top of that, but we are not equipped to do that. [1N4A]

***

The gaps that I see is sometimes the current relevancy of the training we have. When new tools, tactics, or even equipment is fielded, and getting the training institutionalized for mass consumption—it is more of a speed thing. When they come up with a tool to do a new mission, getting training for a new tool is difficult. Technology is evolving more quickly than we can develop the training for it. A lot of the training on the foundational stuff, if we talk about routing and switching, instead of talking about specific products. We talk about the principles of routing and switching, in teaching our airmen how to exploit or defend, regardless of the platforms. Every now and then, there are new platforms that are hard to get into the schoolhouse. There are certainly gaps, but they open and close at a rapid pace. [1B4]

Participants also noted that the equipment used in cyber training might be outdated.

When I was in tech school, there is a range there that contractors maintain, and they mention things about it. A lot of the stuff we are using, it's outdated. [Operations] systems will be out of version. They are struggling to update ranges and keep them functioning. [1B4]

***

51

There is a lot standing in the way to getting it [to] that point. The Air Force in general is too rigid for the dynamic environment that is cyber. The information and skills that we need . . . I was doing a job other than cyber for a year; coming off of not doing that, I was so far behind. We constantly need to be doing the training, changes in skills. There is so much red tape in the way of changing our training that we can't keep up with it. Just going through the initial training—stuff that we covered in initial training is possibly years behind what is actually on the enterprise side because of AETC and AFSPC [Air Force Space Command], the way they have to write the training. In ACC now, what is required to write the course [is] you have to follow this specific structure; we have to cover the legal, the squadron makeup and then eventually we get to cyber skills, but, because of these constructs, there is no flexibility for the training we require on a daily basis. It's not dynamic enough. [1B4]

***

By the time our students are actually taught this information, you are years behind. You are teaching theory that is several years behind [where] the commercial side is. In our current environment, especially the dynamic environment that is cyber, we are automatically having our personnel years behind other countries, and it's not a good thing. [1B4]

***

Not in that space. There are some things that are the quick places where I would look at improving things. There are things that I think we can do that are not heavy lifts that can make big impacts, particularly with the ability to change course work needs to be quicker. The policy is geared to be risk [averse], but I think they create more risk than they mitigate, particularly when they start talking about the difficulty the schoolhouses have in changing topics and criteria. If you look at a university, I can change it semester to semester. Keesler has to go through a big approval chain through a bunch of ropes of management, which probably provides no value in the execution of the task. [SME]

***

Compared to my previous jobs, I did generally the same type of thing the first part of my career, 2003 to 2012; I focused on one thing. I knew that in and out. Not many people knew more than me than my target. In cyber, it's tough to be that one person. It constantly changes. An F-16 doesn't change too much. You can know everything about an F-16 and feel comfortable being an expert. In cyber, if you take one week off, you're probably behind. [1N4A]

***

These skills that you are taught for cyber are not good after a certain amount of time because things change so fast. Unless you are collaborating and continuing to learn and figuring out ways to get at things, it's just so hard. [Workforce—other]

***

Also, a huge lag between what the field is doing [and] how fast the schoolhouse can update its curriculum. As an instructor, within six months the way that they were doing business had completely changed, and then you find out that the information that you are feeding is now out of date. Here, we are constantly changing the software we are using—the interfaces change, the versions get updated. There is not a good mechanism to make sure as soon as this changes, that information is being fed to the schoolhouses to update. Being an instructor, updating curriculum is a pain. [1B4]

## Administrative Red Tape Limits Course Design and Approval

In a number of contexts, participants brought up the burdensome and time-intensive approval processes that limit changes to training. Many participants shared that this issue is a driving factor behind training not reflecting current cyber developments.

The bulk of these comments surfaced in discussions with 1B4s. Related comments made by 1N4As were qualitatively similar but much less frequent.

> I went through training courses. . . . It takes so long to get a course through in the Air Force. By the time it is vetted and approved and funded, it is irrelevant; cyber works so fast. The basics are great; they don't change very often. But the way we move cyber has to be a little faster. We need to get the training to the people faster while it is still relevant. Generally, course approval—you get it vetted by SMEs, all the MAJCOMs [major commands], takes about a year before it rolls out. It is not as current by then. Both OCO and DCO. [1N4A]

***

> I have heard issues at CWO where they have people who do not want to change things even if they have the power to do it. [1B4]

***

> CWO [IQT] was slightly more relevant for defensive operators. I have friends who are instructors, and they want to update, but it takes a long time for AETC to do it, and it's all about pass rates for AETC. [1B4]

***

> So, we did look into getting some systems from the 346th. But that is a network connection, and the connectivity is kind of shoddy. But there were also some complications on what level of administrative privileges we would even have and each level. [1B4]

***

> We have the equipment; it just takes so long to get everything up and running that it loses its value. If I'm going on a mission and I require last-minute training, for them to spin up something to be trained on it, it is going to take well beyond the time that I required it. [1B4]

***

> [To make training that is comparable to the Joint Targeting School Staff Course], we would have to find some way to get it blessed by CYBERCOM. But if we can pull [in an] instructor . . . and start training our folks locally . . . . [But] they just started denying, so I don't even know if we can [train our folks locally] right now. [They started denying] equivalency for some courses. . . . They just said, "We are not doing those anymore." That was meant to help us bridge gaps, plan training out, and get to the FOC [full operational capability] cut. We passed the

FOC cut, so we are not going to entertain that anymore; now you are going to have to go through your pipeline courses and complete your JQS [job qualification standard]. [1B4]

One participant noted that external hurdles push internal training development.

AETC rules for including new curriculum [are] really slow. It takes them a long time to onboard new training material. It has to be revalidated by AETC to get new curriculum approved. We end up building our new training internally. [1B4]

# 5. Appropriateness and Length of the Training Pipeline

This chapter elaborates on participants' comments relating to the broad topic area of the appropriateness and length of the training pipeline. Figure 5.1 contains the issues that were raised by participants in more than three focus groups, and Figure 5.2 contains a related solution that was suggested by participants in more than three groups. The issues raised in Figure 5.1, along with the suggestion to restructure training, are discussed in the remainder of this chapter.

**Figure 5.1. What Needs to Be Improved in Training: Appropriateness and Length of Training Pipeline**

| | Percentage of Focus Groups |
|---|---|
| **Length of Training or Training Pipeline Is Not Appropriate** | |
| Length of training or the pipeline is not appropriate* | 57% |
| Skills atrophy after training | 30% |
| Training redundancy* | 30% |
| Breadth of current training is a problem | 27% |
| Training requirements ignore airmen's current skill background | 20% |
| Cross-training presents challenges* | 20% |
| Development path is ambiguous | 13% |

NOTE: For some topics, no opposite sentiment was expressed in the workforce discussions. Where an opposite sentiment was expressed in 3 to 7 percent of the workforce focus groups (i.e., one or two groups), the category is marked with an asterisk. Percentages represent the number of focus groups in which a topic was mentioned by at least one person. All percentages are out of a total of 30 discussions.

**Figure 5.2. Workforce's Suggested Training Solutions and Changes: Training Structure**

| Training Structure | |
|---|---|
| Overall, training should be structured differently | 30% |

NOTE: No opposite sentiment was offered. Percentages represent the number of focus groups in which a topic was mentioned by at least one person. All percentages are out of a total of 30 discussions.

## The Length of Training or the Training Pipeline Is Not Appropriate, and Training Is Redundant

### *The Length of Training or the Training Pipeline Is Not Appropriate*

In the majority of our discussions, participants brought up issues with the length of training for cyber operators. For both IST and the entire pipeline, participants expressed dissatisfaction with the time it takes to complete training. Particularly, 1B4 defensive cyber operators remarked that the initial training was too fast, which prevented trainees from being properly taught and decreased retention.

> Some of it was teaching it too fast. We had this one block that was ten days long; you are learning two different systems—a command line, windows, and Linux—and you had five project checks and two tests in ten days. We lost four people out of 12. [1B4]

***

> To develop a good operator, it takes about two years. And this is just from sitting in an organization and watching it happen. I think that the lack of knowledge in developing operators is making it so that we are pushing people faster. The work of an operator takes learning concepts and connecting them to each other. [It] takes time to learn these concepts and connect them together to apply [them]. [1B4]

***

> Lots of info in a short amount of time. The Air Force wants their personnel trained as fast as possible in a field like this. I think more time is needed to really process and apply this material. My school was six months long, and it felt really crammed and rushed. The desire is to have personnel faster. You win and lose. [1B4]

While these defensive operators commented on initial training being too fast-paced, 1B4s and 1N4As from both the offensive and defensive sides described the overall pipeline as taking too long. This can discourage operators who spend a significant amount of time training without opportunities to become involved in actual cyber operations.

> When they are in the role, the last three years, when cyber teams just stand up—people think they are going straight to work, but the first 1.5 years is just training and no operations. That hurts retention. [1N4A]

***

> In the training pipeline, it takes a long time. People show up after UCT, and then they are waiting three to six months before they go in to IQT in JBSA, which is a two- to three-month course. Then, if they can go right to CVAH [Cyberspace Vulnerability Assessment/Hunter course, IQT], which is more, they are qualified, that is another two months. And sometimes they can't even go straight there. We have six to eight months of just them in training; then they come back here and get another class before we can evaluate them. Then, they aren't even fully qualified until we can evaluate them. You are looking at a possible year. With

officers, they can be here between two to three years, and that is half their time. Enlisted, it is [a] quarter of their time. We have people leaving after three years because they spend a year in training, the next year figuring out operations, and then, that last year, they are sort of operating and getting tasks, and then they are good. [1B4]

As one participant described, the length of the training pipeline can also be taxing on operators who have to move to different locations to attend the necessary courses.

If you are moving your family around every six months. You travel to do different types of training. For 1B, it's retrain-only; if the person is coming from [a] cyber background, it is less than six months for IQT, but, if not, they have to go through extra training and its PCS [permanent change of station, meaning move from one assignment to the next], and the family moves to Keesler and then Texas if they go . . . the OCO route to train for six or nine month[s], and then, potentially, they will get an assignment. It is a lot of moving and training. On defense, it is the same at Keesler, but they don't have to go to the six-month pipeline; they have to go to weapons-specific training for three to four months. It is disruptive to family life. [1N4A]

### Training Is Redundant

The training pipeline provides cyber operators with opportunities to take many courses, but some participants criticized the trainings as being too redundant. In some discussions, participants talked about feeling like they had taken multiple courses that covered the same topics or topics that they already knew. Participants described feeling like they were wasting time learning the same thing over and over. They discussed continuation trainings that are too similar to courses found in the initial training pipeline and operators studying topics they already knew. These sentiments were expressed by 1B4s and 1N4As on both the offensive and the defensive sides and were raised about a wide variety of courses. The following are some examples:

A lot of the continuation training is really repetitive. . . . Keesler is a lot of fundamentals, then you go to the initial qualification training, and 60 percent to 80 percent of that was the same information. After that, the Keesler training was four to six months, then the initial qualification training was another three or four months, and 80 percent of that was redundant information. Then, after that, I went to this DCITA [Defense Cyber Investigations Training Academy] that was three months long, and that whole three months was redundant information of the prior two courses. The only new information that I learned was stuff that I went out of my way to learn while I was in those courses. It was repetitive and redundant and a huge waste of time. [1B4]

\*\*\*

JCAC . . . when I went through 2016–2017, awesome. No issues. It was challenging. It was very beneficial. But the testing out of things, when you get here, there are all these different courses you can take. I shouldn't have to take six prereqs to take the one class that I need. That one class that I need is going to benefit me so much more than prereqs. And the prereqs, I probably already learned about at JCAC. [1N4A]

*\*\**

CWOT [CWO course, IQT]—it was very redundant; tech was pretty good for basic skills. Covered a good basis. Go to CWOT, but it was more of a rehash, waste of time. [1B4]

*\*\**

When I went through, it was INWT [Intermediate Network Warfare Training—the predecessor course to CWO, IST], it was the opposite. . . . Used to be UCT at Lackland, and then INWT, and that has changed. UCT had very little tech, and you learned a little at Hurlburt. You missed what the Air Force did offensively. I hear those two schoolhouses would never talk. They would steal from each other. It is two different MAJCOMs that teach, so there is a lot of redundancy because they do not talk to each other. [1B4]

Participants elaborated on why repetition was occurring, pointing to obstacles in communication and information-sharing across the schoolhouses. They talked about how the same range technology and course curriculum are being developed by scratch in multiple places because that information is owned and developed by contractors and subject to copyright or other contractual restrictions that permit its use in only one location. They also talked about how no single entity is overseeing the training pipeline to create an overarching plan for how each course is intended to build on others and to eliminate overlap in course content. Participants gave examples in which course information was sometimes shared among MAJCOMs and schoolhouses because of existing relationships among those involved. Participants said that it would be better if communication could be more formalized and institutionalized so that it endures when new personnel come into the schoolhouses. A few participants noted that training redundancy could also be useful in some circumstances because it could help reinforce the training content, but, in those cases, redundancy should be intentional rather than haphazard and accidental.

## Skills Atrophy After Initial Training

Focus group participants spoke of the need for continual technical engagement to keep their cyber skills from atrophying.[39] We heard several references to two particular situations that likely lead to skills atrophying: being assigned to a role that does not leverage one's cyber training and being "pulled off keyboard" through promotion. 1N4As, 1B4s, and civilians articulated similar concerns about skills atrophying. Concerns about atrophy after promotion to leadership arose among 1N4As.

---

[39] This concern about skill atrophy also comes up in other career fields (e.g., intel and linguistics).

I have had leadership say your skills don't atrophy, but, if you talk to anyone on the job . . . if I take leave for two weeks, I am rusty. I don't know how people go two years not touching anything. [1N4A]

*** 

Being out for 18 months, it's going to be hard for me to take a tech assessment. [1B4]

*** 

Just practicing and having hands on keyboard is vital. Like languages, if you don't use it, it's gone. If you aren't practicing and doing these things, it goes away. And then you fail out of training and get sent to twiddle your thumbs until you can go back to the same training. [1B4]

*** 

I took a significant pay cut to go become an AGR [Active Guard Reserve] because I saw it as a training opportunity. I thought I could do it for three years, and I'm going to get all sorts of training that the contract won't pay for. And I think I was a little mistaken. The reserves don't really pay for training; the active-duty guys will go to vendor training and will get specialized training. But they do not want to pay for reservists. I never got a clear answer. I tried to go to the training that the active duty goes to. . . . I get rustier and rustier. I have lost a ton of skills. It was a big mistake coming here for the last two years. I feel like I have lost a lot of my abilities. [1B4]

Although the above comment highlights the possibility that Active Guard Reserve personnel might face potential atrophy as a result of decreased access to training relative to active-duty personnel, we cannot say whether the issue with access to training for those groups is widespread, because we do not have a sufficient number of Active Guard Reserve personnel in our sample to make such a comparison. That said, it is worth noting that this example is one way that skills might be atrophying.

Atrophy can also occur if a cyber assignment neglects to leverage skills acquired during initial training.

I don't know if there is so much of a training issue as there is an atrophy issue. We can send folks to classes constantly; if they are not using the skills, then you are just going to have to constantly resend them [to training]. [1N4A]

*** 

In a lot of cases, you start all over, and you can be completely misutilized and have atrophy of skills, especially for our 1N4As. If you are assigned to [an] NSA mission and they have a role called exploit analysts, they go through a significant pipeline. If you are NSA or CYBERCOM, they have a pipeline. [Workforce— other]

Being pulled off keyboard can also result in the atrophying of key cyber skills.

Once people start making rank . . . [skills atrophying] is another big issue. . . . You get these admin roles, and your cyber skill set will depreciate because you will not use it. [1N4A]

I've been doing the job longer than most EAs I know. About a year ago, I finally got promoted. I stepped away from the keyboard the last six months. I have no idea what is going on anymore. It takes that quick for you to lose that skill set. . . . The reason my skills were so sharp up to that point was because I kept being sent to classes; I was continuing to do the job they paid me to do without being pulled to do all this red tape stuff. [1N4A]

## The Breadth of Current Training Is a Problem

Some participants expressed the view that cyber training often attempts to teach too much information in a limited amount of time. As a result, operators attempt to learn a large amount of information on multiple topics, which prevents them from becoming experts in certain topics. Furthermore, given the broad variety of topics, instructors might not be able to effectively teach the material. This issue was brought up in approximately one-quarter of our discussions.

The amount of info you have to swallow to put on a test is insurmountable. The training is not where it should be. A class will give you an overview, maybe like key words, but it does not teach you how to do the job. It simply teaches you about the job. If you cannot do daily training as an operator of what you are doing every day, then people start forgetting what they learned. [1B4]

***

You are being taught all these things, and they expect you to know everything, but you are only a specialist in one. You don't do eye surgery in the morning [and] then go work on brain surgery while you are looking at someone's feet in the afternoon. We are expected to be broad. Cyber is very, very broad. [1B4]

***

We are expected to know [it] all. We are given very little continuous training after we leave tech school. We get some commercial, if someone can find it. Or, when a mission comes up around one topic, we try to scrape together a training for one thing—but it is not continuous. [1B4]

***

It's good. It can be done better. . . . You can't teach programming language in four hours. . . . People are struggling, and the pressure is intense. . . . It can be done without their suffering, but it takes time. For someone who has had basic computer science training, they still need to know how it is done in cyber. [Civilian]

## Training Requirements Ignore Airmen's Current Skill Backgrounds

Participants shared feedback that the backgrounds and skill sets of airmen are not taken into consideration prior to their attending a class. This one-size-fits-all approach potentially creates training redundancy (an issue described in a prior section). Participants from 1B4 and the civilian workforce shared these concerns.

I would also say, speed of need, learning things and assessing people up front. Every individual is different; what works for one is not going to work for all. That's a problem that we have in the DoD; we blanket-approach, so you have a lot of people coming into this career field that have years of networking background, but we make them still go through networking. People that are ex-programmers, and we are going to make them do weeks of programing. Not all people have those same backgrounds, but we apply the same training across the board. I have a lot of respect for the ex-maintainers that we have a lot of; they are coming in with no background, except maybe personal experience. But then other people [are] coming in with networking background, so the schoolhouse seems boring to those people in some aspects and just right for someone coming in with no experience. So, having it more tailored. Just having a one size fits all is hindering us now. [1B4]

## 1B4 Being a Cross-Train-Only Career Field Presents Challenges

1B4 historically has been a cross-train-only, or retrain-only, career field. That rule was changed only recently, in 2019. At the time this study was conducted, only a few 1B4 personnel had entered into the career field at accession. Given that our discussions took place only a few months after the first person straight from accession had entered the career field (see Bui, 2019), the overwhelming majority of participants in our 1B4 discussions would have been cross-train-only (and it is likely that all of them were). During our discussions, this change in policy was raised by a number of our 1B4 participants, and they noted that it might have bearing on the training needs and issues in a variety of ways.

For example, 1B4 participants talked about the challenges of the career field being "cross-train-only." 1B4s had historically been cross-trained from other career fields only. That is, they had all been in USAF serving in other career fields when they applied or were recruited into cyber. In this way, 1B4s were entering the career field as more-senior airmen transferring in from another career field, which is sometimes referred to as *lateral entry.*

One concern about the 1B4 career field being retrain-only was that it often presents a barrier to entry for interested individuals. A 1B4 shared,

> You hear about this career field, you're excited, but you can't join it until you get in and then retrain, since it's retrain-only. . . . If that's still the model they are talking about through the recruiters, then that is going to be difficult to find people to bring in. That's an obstacle. [1B4]

Interested individuals might not ultimately make it into the career field because they lose momentum or skills during their initial assignments.

Cross-training might be more or less of a challenge depending on where an individual is coming from.

> If you were a 3D, you already have pretty much gone through the whole gamut of training. You already have security plus at that point. For someone who is cross-training from a completely different career field, it's like dropping a bomb on

them. They have to learn all that in a matter of a week and a half and pass to be able to continue. [1B4]

Lack of prior operational cyber experience combined with gaps in training makes retraining an obstacle to effectiveness.

> Yes, for a long time, it was a retrain-only career field [with] people coming from maintenance, security forces, finance. They don't have an operational background. But when you go to an actual [operations] squadron, they go through operational-type instruction, and we don't get that in cyber. So, they come in with mostly a maintenance perspective rather than an operations perspective, so it's hard for them to transition. We are not as effective as we could be if we were given that type of training. [1B4]

Participants are also concerned that being retrain-only contributes to the acceleration of initial cyber training, and that also might be contributing to a number of the challenges associated with teaching and coursework described earlier in this chapter. For example, one participant explained that, instead of training to be developers over the course of their first two years, cyber operators and analysts must go through intensive, accelerated training.

> Because we do cross-train-only, that takes off that first couple of years that we could have been teaching someone to be a developer. Then we have this guy that's trying to learn it, boot camp style, but I don't think that's the best way to build out a lasting force. [1B4]

An additional obstacle presented by cross-training is that the timing of initial cyber training has to align well with an airman's term to facilitate the transition. If there are limited places in training or an airman's availability is not well aligned to the training schedule, then that individual might not successfully navigate to the new career field.

> When I went through [training], they had a shortfall program because it was critically manned. It was relatively easy to go through the process of cross-training. . . . But . . . I think it's kind of egregious for second term up airmen because there is a different process for having to go through that. . . . There [are] windows of opportunity to cross-train that [are] a little more limited because you only have so many slots that you have available to people who can cross-train versus shortfalls. You are kind of a special case. [1B4]

Participants also recognized various benefits of cross-training into the cyber career fields, including that cross-training leads to higher-quality operators and analysts compared with those in the equivalent career field in other services and in other USAF career fields.

> Our folks tend to be older, too. They are not learning the military at the same time they are going through the course. The 1B4s cross-train, and they already know how to be in the Air Force; they are able to just focus on the course. The other services . . . sometimes, they will get that guy straight out of boot camp, goes right to his tech school, goes right here, gets to be in civilian clothes for seven months to a year and a half. It's a different viewpoint. [1B4]

Participants' explanations for the differences in quality focused on the knowledge, experience, and maturity of the operators and the process of weeding out those who are ill-suited to the career field. Participants raised the point that cross-training begets maturity and relevant noncyber experience. One 1B4 explained that

> because we're a cross-trained-only career field, we tend to be older, more mature, and a lot of people have more experience that doesn't necessarily come from cyber. When we talk to other organizations that we work with, they're like, "When we get an Air Force guy, we know that we're going to get a different quality of person than a guy straight out of Navy basic training." [1B4]

Additionally, cross-training can serve to weed out those who are interested but might be ill-suited to the rigor of the career field. Navigating the logistical process to apply for and enroll in training might keep less dedicated would-be cyber operators and analysts from entering the field. One 1B4 said, "There are people that are interested in it, but, if they don't have the follow-through to apply for cross-training, then I don't know if they would be set up well to participate in the career field" [1B4]. However, the barrier of this logistical burden might also prevent individuals who would make strong cyber operators and analysts from being able to contribute to the field.

## The Development Path Is Ambiguous

In some discussions, participants expressed the view that the training pipeline is unclear or poorly structured. Airmen felt that the progression ladder for cyber personnel should be more clearly defined and explained.

> We need to do a better job with the development track and lay out a way ahead for people in their development. You could easily get lost in the shuffle if you don't sit down and go over your track. [1N4A]

## Some Participants Suggested that Training Should Be Structured Differently Overall

During some discussions, participants suggested that changes to the overall approach and structure of training were needed. Suggestions included a more formal training structure that identifies the specific skill path required to complete the mission and a plan to develop and advance the skills of the workforce. Participants also suggested changing how training content is managed and updated, including having a regular review of training, having a formal process for inventorying new technologies acquired, and developing training for new cyber personnel to keep pace with the changing nature of the cyber field.

> [Training] should be more frequent. If we fix some of these other things, like getting it more relevant and not being dated, . . . then [after IST] it should be very planned that there is a frequency for more advanced training. Obviously, a lot of things would have to be answered, like, what is advanced, and is it advanced based on where you are at. . . . Here, I think it would be great to teach somebody initial skills—skills that have to do with analysis, wire shark and what TCPIP

[Transmission Control Protocol/Internet Protocol] packets are, how to analyze traffic. Then, two or three years later, come back . . . and go a little bit deeper into some of those protocols. But, right now, it's complete Wild West as to what courses we go and take for that advanced training, and everybody is doing something different. [1B4]

# 6. Training Ownership and Utilization of Personnel

This chapter provides participants' comments relating to the broad topic area of issues with training ownership and utilization of personnel. Comments about these issues and related solutions suggested by participants in more than three focus groups are shown in Figures 6.1 and 6.2, respectively.

**Figure 6.1. What Needs to Be Improved in Training: Training Ownership and Utilization of Personnel**

| | Percentage of Focus Groups |
|---|---|
| **Training Ownership Presents Issues** | |
| Squadrons are designing unit training and this is a problem | 37% |
| The Air Force does not have proper ownership of training | 27% |
| **Utilization of Personnel** | |
| Personnel prefer to stay on keyboard (related to development) | 60% |
| Cyber personnel are misutilized or ineffectively utilized | 43% |
| Knowledge gap is created when airmen are moved | 23% |

NOTE: No opposite sentiment was offered. Percentages represent the number of focus groups in which a topic was mentioned by at least one person. All percentages are out of a total of 30 discussions.

**Figure 6.2. Workforce's Suggested Training Solutions and Changes: Training Ownership**

| | |
|---|---|
| **Training Ownership Suggestions** | |
| More Air Force ownership of training would be beneficial* | 30% |
| Commercial or public training options would be beneficial | 27% |

NOTE: Where an opposite sentiment was expressed in 3 to 7 percent of the workforce focus groups (i.e., one or two groups), the category is marked with an asterisk. Percentages represent the number of focus groups in which a topic was mentioned by at least one person. All percentages are out of a total of 30 discussions.

## Training Ownership

### Problems Arise from Squadrons Designing Unit Training

After initial training, cyber operators often desire more continuation training to better fit the needs of the unit and mission. Although there are opportunities for operators to seek out formalized courses, some participants indicated that their units developed their own unique trainings. Operators described frustrations with the need to teach their units certain topics that ideally would be covered in formalized courses; they also described a lack of direction in creating training. With little guidance and formal support, these participants report feeling as though they are spending more time than they should be teaching operators to do their jobs. This topic arose in nearly 40 percent of our discussions and was found across specialty areas and career fields. Instances of participants discussing the lack of training guidance include the following:

> We do not have training standards, so, if you have a team where everyone gets moved around, and a certain group and it worked, you cannot move certain people, [be]cause then you have huge gaps. Not defining training is an issue we run into. We stopped looking above for any sort of direction for what we should be doing. We just do it on our own on the team level. It has been so many years waiting for someone up high to give us direction, and it does not come, so we just do it on our own. [Civilian]

***

> I have seen this a few times, where people come into the unit and they are new and see people who want training of things, and they start up an internal squad training program where they are training on cool stuff, and then they get bored and move on. Then, that disappears. When it's there, it's cool, and people say good things. But [it's] so informal and person-dependent that it never keeps going, and it depends on what they personally have access to that gives you that training. It would be better if it was more formalized and had more training. [1N4A]

***

> It wasn't based on the Air Force direction. It was the commander who said they needed their people to be better at their job. It is up to the individual unit to figure it out. If there was a push from the higher level that said, "OK, here is a baseline for your people to meet." It should not be up to the commander to find the money. It should be, "Here is money for you to send your people to training, to set a standard." [1N4A]

***

> As for the continuation training at the unit, it seems like there are things that people have built [or] set up as training, but it is not set up in a formal way or advertised to the operators in whole. [1B4]

Participants also noted that some of the unit-designed training primarily teaches operators about topics that they should already know from previous training.

> Our formalized training is that you usually get someone from tech school; it doesn't teach you how to do your job, just, "Do you have the aptitude?" So, even after we have people from these schoolhouses, we still have to take them and actually train them on their job. For that week, year, they are specializing, but, the next week, you have more information. When they finish schoolhouse, they retain maybe 10 to 20 percent. [1B4]

***

There are drawbacks to mission effectiveness. We're designed to train to maintain currency and advance proficiency. Folks should already have the basics, but we have to go back and provide training on topics that should have been covered. [1B4]

### USAF Does Not Have Proper Ownership of Needed Additional Training

In their discussion of challenges related to training, participants from the 1B4 and 1N4A career fields articulated the view that USAF does not have appropriate ownership of additional training opportunities that serve to develop critical depth and expertise in cyber.[40] This challenge came up in roughly one-quarter of the focus groups.

Participants talked about the lack of responsibility for and control over standards, which leads to lackluster training outcomes.

The Air Force is not responsible for the training I did; they let me TDY. For us currently, it's U.S. Cyber Command who handles that. They contract that out to a contractor who contracts that out to another contractor. . . . I think that's absolutely a problem. My personal opinion, I think the service components should know about the standards set. We'll get to the standard, but it'll be harder to get there, and [we] cannot control our seat slots and have to divide amongst people. If they just gave them the standards, the Air Force could teach to it. But now, the Air Force does not have the control for it. [1B4]

During discussions of training ownership, participants proposed that USAF bring contracted or NSA training in-house because of concerns about problems with current course capacity, relevance of training to USAF tools and capabilities, and overall training quality.

Participants identified particular courses or pieces of training that USAF should bring in house, including technical capabilities and NSA job role training.

We absolutely need better training for technical capabilities. . . . The Air Force needs to own more on the technical capabilities because we don't organically have or own anything (e.g., SEC 660, advanced exploitation course). We're just buying it. [1B4]

***

[To improve training], there needs to be Air Force training that trains qualifications for an NSA job role. They are trying to do that; they're bringing in more instructors. So NCS [National Cryptologic School] is the school [inside the NSA] that teaches all NSA courses, and they are trying to bring in more

---

[40] Note that the training referenced as not currently belonging to USAF (training that is owned by U.S. Cyber Command or NSA) reflects training that USAF personnel are saying is needed to build depth of technical expertise in advanced areas. If owned by USAF, that training likely would be expected to occur after IST as part of the continuation training pipeline or as a form of career development and not during or as part of the IST pipeline. However, if such additional training opportunities were owned by USAF, they could also consider adding some elements of that training to IST to help further develop depth of skills before airmen reach their first assignments.

instructors to be able to teach more classes to enable more Air Force billeted personnel to take more courses. [1N4A]

Airmen also expressed concerns about the product-oriented approach of contracted training courses. One 1N4A remarked that external training is sometimes part of a marketing plot that results in suboptimal transferability of knowledge, skills, and abilities (KSAs).

> When we utilize civilian training, oftentimes that training is to teach you how to use a tool that they are kind of selling or that they use. But that tool may not be the tool you actually use in your work environment. So, instead of gaining 100 percent—"I got trained on this, and now I can do it"—you only take away about 50 percent of it, and you kind of see how it does the same thing [as the tool you do have access to]. So, we need to be cautious on the selection of civilian courses to ensure we maximize transferable KSAs. [1N4A]

Participants also expressed the view that USAF-owned training might lead to better retention by limiting the number of civilian certifications that airmen have and their knowledge of the transferability and payoff of their skills in the civilian labor force.

> We rely on civilian certifications to train our people. They are the closest fit to what we do and the skill sets we have. Rather than train to what we have, we train to industry standards. What it does is make our airmen marketable. . . . They can stay in as an E5 or easily get out and make easily about $150K per year. . . . It's easy to get those jobs based on what we provided them. We give them every excuse to leave. [1N4A]

It is interesting to note that participants' view that there should be more USAF-owned training might appear to run counter to the following section, which suggests that private or commercial training would be helpful. However, these two ideas might not be mutually exclusive. There could be a benefit to having both more USAF-owned training in certain areas and more access to some of the high-quality, off-the-shelf commercial or private-sector training.

### Provide Commercial or Public Training Options for Ongoing Training

In 27 percent of focus groups, participants advocated for the provision of ongoing training using commercial or public training options rather than in-house USAF training. Some relevant training is now available in the public domain.[41]

> The civilian part of this we need to be able to leverage because the universities are teaching basically the same stuff. We have our own spin on things, but all this

---

[41] By *training in the public domain*, we mean the type of training that would be available in private-sector training (proprietary or not) or in university settings (e.g., advanced theory and applied training on how to defend against attacks) as opposed to the kind of training that might be available only to the military (i.e., training in offensive and warfare types of activities). Note that training available in the public domain might be limited as a result (e.g., it might provide only basic cyber skills, including coding, capture-the-flag exercises, and establishing defensive capabilities). Because of legal restrictions and policy, pure OCO would not be available in the public domain unless specific legal elements were applied under ethical hacker training or penetration testing—and this likely would be only through private-sector training.

information is out there in the public domain. We should be taking advantage of that as well. [1B4]

Proponents of private-sector training emphasized the customizability of such options.

> For us, we look for private sector industry-standard training and go for it. In fact, a lot of squadrons do that. It ends up being self-paced, squadron-crafted, or "purchased training." [1B4]

Other participants reported different experiences with commercial providers and warned that private-sector providers do not want to customize, but they instead want to fit their existing training into a (perhaps unaligned) USAF need.

> A lot of vendors out there have these templates that they just sell to everybody. There is no good vendor that is selling exactly something for, especially if it's a merge between analysts and operators, taking data and being able to not just solve a technical problem but work through that whole process. I know the Air Force has asked for that, but I think a lot of times the vendors, "Oh, yeah. That sounds great; we understand what your needs are and what you want to be trained against. But here's Netwars [a set of scenarios and a range owned and operated by the commercial company SANS Institute]; go ahead and buy this for $200K." [Workforce—other]

Some participants highlighted commercial partners who provide customized, quality training options. Booz Allen Hamilton and SANS Institute came up multiple times.

> Booz Allen Hamilton is working on the new range and is almost finished with it. When it is up and running, it will be great. [1B4]

> \*\*\*

> That is step 1: Give us collegiate-level training. Then, provide more support and resources to Booz or whoever is building the range. [1B4]

> \*\*\*

> Additional courses depending on what they would be doing. In our squadron, we are afforded those additional opportunities if we want to go through different SANS courses that would be beneficial to our career, if we can make that judgment to our leadership to get more people in that class, building up the weak areas for each individual. [1B4]

> \*\*\*

> SANS courses are always very good, or CompTIA certifications. (Security+ was a CompTIA certification.)[42] SANS courses are really amazing—the one thing I liked during CWO. They actually had a SANS instructor come in and [do] a SANS course. It was a forensics course, not relevant to OCO. But it helped to know that, after an incident happens, they will come and pull the hard drive and . . . how they could discover how a network was compromised. There are completely different SANS courses that are beneficial for OCO [and] DCO. They

---

[42] CompTIA is a commercial training provider for Security+.

have a reverse-engineering class; certified ethical hacker courses would be good. [1B4]

One participant advocated for a wholesale restructuring of initial cyber training that leverages commercial options instead of in-house training.

> I want to make this clear—I think we need to take commercial-type training and use that for the Air Force, not take it and put it in the Air Force, because, then, we use the Air Force mechanism to do training. I go to Keesler for IST, and it is block training and the old way of [training]. We have always done this instead of online. Commercial training is so much better than [what USAF provides]. I go back to saying it is archaic because that is exactly how it is perceived. [1B4]

Some advocated for leveraging the private sector to improve training overall.

> In the cyber world . . . there is an expectation of a correlation between the industry and military that does not occur. The private sector should be used as a roadmap and could help with our gaps. [1B4]

## Utilization of Personnel

### *Personnel Are Misutilized or Ineffectively Utilized*

As shown in Figure 6.3, overall, participants reported that their skills and training were not being well utilized.[43] 1B4s responded with only slight agreement on average when asked whether their skills were utilized well in their unit and their talents were used well in the workplace. More specifically, the mean response was close to halfway between a 3 (neither agree nor disagree) and a 4 (somewhat agree). This suggests that 1B4 participants think that there is still considerable room for improvement in the utilization of their skills. Civilians tended to be a little more positive than the 1B4s. In contrast, on these same questions, 1N4As tended to be only slightly dissatisfied with how personnel are utilized.

This general topic of misutilization of personnel also came up in 43 percent of our discussions (see Figure 6.1). Participants from all three career fields offered a variety of comments that provide additional context. For example, because of the ever-changing nature of the field, effective talent management was seen as necessary but lacking.

> Are all cyber personnel utilized as intended? No. I would say I was in a unit for two years where cyber personnel were not being utilized for cyber functions. . . . I went through JCAC and had all these skills, but a good chunk of my tour was to Google current events on anything cyber-related and brief that to a 20-member meeting. If you look at what we are trained to do and what we did, I would say it was a misutilization. . . . We always cry about manning, but it sounds funny if

---

[43] Note that the issue of misutilization of personnel not only relates to the topic of training but also was discussed by our participants as a potential driver of retention. Therefore, we include this section of results in both this volume and Volume II of this report.

you say we need to produce more but we have them and don't know how to use them. [SME]

**Figure 6.3. Average Responses to Questions About Utilization of Talent**

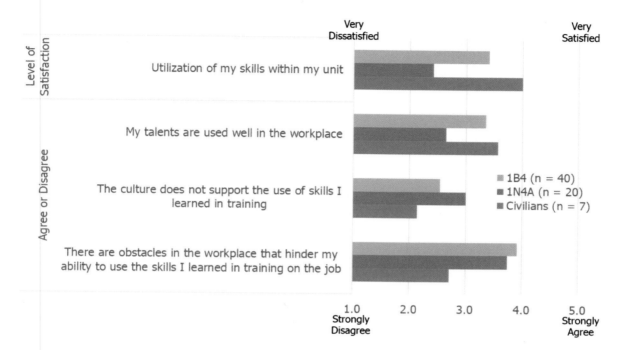

In addition, some participants suggested using a better talent management system for 1B4s, providing personnel with more-relevant work assignments, putting more effort into assigning personnel to work roles depending on which skills they need to develop, rotating personnel more often, and making work roles more clearly defined.

*Moving Airmen Creates a Knowledge Gap*

As shown in Figure 6.1, participants in 23 percent of groups also talked about how a knowledge gap is created when airmen are moved. Because of the length of time that it takes to train cyber personnel, it takes a long time to regain the skills and knowledge that are lost because of airmen being moved around or leaving USAF. This type of knowledge gap is especially pronounced when one of the field's small number of high performers leaves or is moved.

> Your best guy is probably five times better than your general adequate performers. You have your superior performers, who are significantly higher performing than those who are just here doing their jobs every day. . . . I don't think the type of work we're doing is something you can throw quantity at. I think that quality wins the war. That one smart guy with the one great idea is going to be the success or failure of what we're doing over the course of a year in a long-term plan. That guy is my concern on the retention incentive. The numbers will look healthy, but when you look at—I think that Sgt. [X] is a great example. That tab that he wears labels him with significant experience. If we lose

71

that, it's going to take another three to five years to build another Sgt [X]. If we lose him to industry, it will significantly adversely impact the way we're able to operate over the long term. [1B4]

*\*\**

The big problem that I see is that you have people get to the point [where] they start contributing around year two or three, and they get moved, and now that skill is lost. [SME]

## Personnel Prefer to Stay on Keyboard

The utilization topic that received the most discussion was the desire to keep personnel on keyboard. As was noted in Chapter 3, participants expressed concern about being taken "off keyboard" as they progress in their careers. As airmen advance in rank, they are expected to take on more managerial or administrative duties at the expense of performing more technical work. Comments in this category pertain to the need for an alternative path for those who do not wish to give up technical work.

There needs to be a point in an operator's career where they can choose to be an operator or stay technical. The Air Force invests a lot in its members, and there comes a time when training is not relevant. Rank becomes more important than the knowledge they hold. We have members who do not want to promote because they do not want to stop what they are doing, and that is just sad. If you have someone with a half-a-million-dollar education, they shouldn't be doing administrative duties; they should be employed the way they were designed to be employed. The Air Force is failing at that. It's sad. [1B4]

Participants suggested that the creation of more-senior technical roles would be advantageous for performance and retention. Suggestions of the need for a technical pathway for promotion arose from discussion related to promotion that necessitates that cyber operators and analysts move off keyboard and into roles that are more focused on management.

Once people start making rank and forcing admin duties, [atrophy of skills] is another big issue. . . . Having a path for people to stay technical while being able to make rank [would be good]. [1N4A]

Participants articulated that the desire to remain technical is often stronger than the desire for promotion. Participants spoke of either explicit efforts to avoid promotion or a disinclination to seek opportunities to be considered for promotion.

I have staff . . . and techs that will go in and Christmas tree their promotion tests so that they don't get promoted,[44] because they know—especially the techs—if they get promoted to master, they know they are done technically. [1N4A]

*\*\**

---

[44] *Christmas tree* refers to an intentional way of responding on a Scantron test; the test-taker fills in the bubbles in a zigzag or random pattern (akin to the outline of a Christmas tree or to decorations on a Christmas tree) to receive a failing score on the test.

I'm definitely that person who wants to stay technical and doesn't want to get pulled into leadership stuff. I'm not saying I'm sandbagging my promotion, because I'm not, but I really don't want to get promoted. [1B4]

***

I'm not going to go out of my way [to earn promotion]. [1B4]

Eventually, the lack of senior-level technical roles leads operators and analysts to leave USAF because of the abundant opportunities to continue to do the technical work elsewhere.

We don't have technical leaders, what we have is technical SMEs who have tech sergeant and below, and they start losing that because they start running things. [1B4]

Participants compared talent management in USAF with the management of senior-level technical experience in industry. Industry cultivates technical depth and respects decisions to remain technical rather than go toward management; USAF values rank over technical depth.

[In industry], if they have someone who is really good at technical ability and doesn't want to go into leadership, . . . that is OK: They can stay and be paid the same. We don't do that. We have tech sergeants who do technical stuff on a network, and they get $60K, and, in industry, it's $250[K]. . . . We value based on their rank, not based on what they bring to the fight. [Workforce—other]

Participants conveyed that this leaky pipeline contributes to "perpetual amateurism" in the squadrons that might be easily remedied by a technically focused track.

If you want to progress to E8 and above, then you have to try to work at . . . the superintendent level. It's all managerial there. There is no more of technically utilizing your skill. If we had a technically focused track, we could maintain a higher level of expertise and grow people so that we don't have perpetual amateurism. [1B4]

Participants noted that the technically oriented senior roles in other services might be well suited to the talent management needs of cyber. In particular, there was discussion of the opportunity for a technical cyber pathway to include the warrant officer role that is more prevalent in other services.

One way to fix that would be warrant officers. Nobody wants to hear it. As warrant officers, we would have the ability to get promoted and to be paid more but wouldn't have to deal with the SNCO admin stuff. [1B4]

Overall, USAF moves individuals around in a way that is suboptimal for talent management, and participants expressed the view that there might be advantages to changing the training and promotion pipelines to better leverage existing talent.

Talent management negatively impacts training. We don't foster skill sets. We move people around randomly, which causes skill attrition every time. You don't see that in industry. We will move them around; one day you are doing X, and the next day you are doing Y—sometimes make them retrain. We chase our own tails a bit. [Workforce—other]

# 7. Other Suggestions for Improvement

In previous chapters, we talked about solutions suggested by participants that were directly relevant to the training issues they raised. However, participants also suggested a few other ways to improve training. Figure 7.1 summarizes the remaining suggestions that were mentioned by more than three groups and were not discussed in any of the previous chapters. Throughout this chapter, we present comments related to these suggestions. In addition, in some discussions, we asked participants directly about their views on the KSAOs needed prior to entering training; their responses are also reported in this chapter. Lastly, we briefly describe a variety of additional miscellaneous suggestions that were offered less frequently (i.e., in three or fewer discussions) than those displayed in Figure 7.1.

**Figure 7.1. Workforce's Suggested Training Solutions and Changes: Better Applicant and Instructor Screening and Modeling the Other Services**

| | Percentage of Focus Groups |
|---|---|
| **Better Instructor and Applicant Screening** | |
| Implement aptitude testing to help find best people* | 33% |
| **Do Something Similar to the Other Services** | |
| Modeling other military services is a good idea** | 47% |

NOTE: Where an opposite sentiment was expressed in 3 to 7 percent of the workforce focus groups (i.e., one or two groups), the category is marked with an asterisk. Where an opposite sentiment was expressed by 10 percent of focus groups (i.e., three groups), the category is marked with two asterisks. Percentages represent the number of focus groups in which a topic was mentioned by at least one person. All percentages are out of a total of 30 discussions.

## Implement Aptitude Testing to Help with Screening

In 33 percent of the focus groups, 1B4, 1N4A, and civilian participants commented on how aptitude testing would help screen individuals entering cyber training; they said that aptitude testing would decrease washout rates and better identify the strengths and weaknesses of incoming trainees. Some participants focused on how the testing could better identify talented individuals and weed out those who do not have the skills to be successful operators. Several examples of these statements are as follows:

> We get a lot of people that go through and they fail out because, I have heard, they are in over their heads, not grasping concepts. Or, we have people who get through but then never get through clearances. A better screening would help a ton. [1N4A]

***

They have to take a test, some cyber test[45]—AFOQT—have to study for it. Why don't we do something, before they come in, where it shows their aptitude. For cyber, if there was a test [that required them] to learn certain aspects of network stuff, where they had to study before to really learn this stuff, and test to get the job—it would take a long time to study and learn. Here are some videos to watch, some materials you can take home with you and study for it and take this day before you come in. Instead of us wasting time and effort to get this person in and then they get washed out, we give them something where they have to do some scripting, or something they have to have a certain level of proficiency with. [1N4A]

***

I think a better screening of the people we choose to send through these courses need[s] to be done. I don't know what it looks like. Not only for aptitude for the courses in the community itself but also things like screening. [1N4A]

***

One of the challenges that DoD has had with cyber, specially 1B4, is with recruitment and finding people who are capable of doing roles we ask. We have been working with partners like [the University] of Maryland [that are] looking at cognitive skill sets to identify people with aptitude to do this work—not all about skills in the past, but finding people who can think in the right way. How do we identify if we can measure it, and what kind of tests do we need to provide? All services are struggling with this. [SME]

Although weeding out poorly performing trainees would be one benefit of aptitude screening, some participants also said they believed that proper testing would be able to suggest career paths that would fit the skills and interests of trainees. With these tests, USAF would be able to tell what trainees are interested in or where they have previous experience. This could improve retention because these individuals would be placed in areas of interest. Participants made the following suggestions:

I wouldn't know how to guide that testing—I don't think that's something the Air Force does a good job of anyway. We have ASVAB [Armed Services Vocational Aptitude Battery], and we have JCAC, but people can make it through that but then be put into [a] job they aren't well suited for. They may have a mind that's better suited for offensive, but they're placed in defensive operations, or vice versa. [1N4A]

***

A better process of placement test that you have to take before you sign up or become a 1N4A. The way we do it now, I don't know the washout rate since JCAC became the AFSC awarding course, so I cannot talk to that right now. But

---

[45] The participant did not specify to which cyber test they were referring. No such cyber test exists on the Air Force Officer Qualifying Test (AFOQT); however, there are minimum AFOQT scores required for entry into the cyber officer AFSs.

75

I know before then [we were not] sending the right people through the course. Logic is one of the blocks, and it gets a lot of people. [1N4A]

***

The one thing I want to bring up is to see where proficiencies are lacking. I might be lacking in network, but I excel in host. I like Windows, so I know where to look for changes; I know what programs to use as they come out. I believe there should be a proficiency test to see where they should track for as it comes along in a career. Instead of being a jack of all trades, you are a master of one. [1B4]

***

If I were going to try to remake the pipeline, I would do—a lot of this stuff is unclassified general knowledge. I know there's some Air Force e-learning, but, if they had a pretest where you had to go through Unix, Windows, networking, and just pass the test on these things with midlevel knowledge—if you passed that, then you could talk to the career-field manager about the career. That would stop people who don't really have the interest or knowledge from taking slots from those who do, and then the actual training wouldn't have to cover that foundational knowledge that they should already have. [1B4]

***

When you start assessing people to go into jobs, we will pick people and say, "OK, we want you to go into this job," and that is what we assess you as, but we really don't know how to per se assess aptitude for topics you have never seen before. You may have airmen show up that may be very, very good at being a cyber operator, but maybe they didn't grow up with computers in their home. You don't know how good they would be without someone to assess—we don't do that today. On the other side of that, we have people that may appear to be good at something because they spent a lot of time on it, but their aptitude is not very high, and their lack of latent skill can catch up in the long run. The means by which we assess the talent needs to be improved. [We] need to make sure those with the right talent [get] into the career field, and [having the right assessment tool can] both make them more successful and make them like it more and enjoy it. [SME]

## Participants Compared USAF Methods with Those of the National Security Agency and the Other Services

When discussing cyber training, many participants compared USAF's training methods and pipeline with those of other cyber entities, including other military services and NSA. The most common policy mentioned by participants was the warrant officer program found in other military services. This was cited as both a potential solution for retention issues among cyber operators (see Volume II of this report) and a suggestion for how to improve training and development of personnel. Examples of the training-related comments include the following:

The Air Force is so against warrant officers, but that is what the other branches do to keep their members who they spent all this money [on] to keep them technical and getting wins in cyber. We don't do that. We see it as, "Cool, we taught them; now, go be a leader." It happens sometimes, but, a lot of times, you will either not make rank or get out for better opportunities. [1B4]

Participants noted that, along with retaining more-experienced operators, other organizations were able to use experienced officers as formal instructors.

> We did something similar in the Navy. I am a big proponent. We give people a group of tasks to complete. We give them a senior person to sign off on those. And they have to take a written and hands-on task to pass each level. Then, at each level, there are harder qualifications. So, you have to do that at each step. Eventually, you're the master, and you teach other people. [1B4]

***

> More adjunct faculty on NSA side. Well, it would be on U.S. CYBERCOM side, or even the Air Force side, to get NSA to authorize adjunct faculty to teach some of the basic classes, or even the more advanced ones. NSA would have to do it, because it's their curriculum. But the Air Force could push it. The Air Force could, for example—I don't know if this is policy, but one of the Army units we work with, the Army civilians have to be adjunct faculty. [Civilian]

***

> Yeah. The Air Force could do something like that, where they open that up. If you're particularly good at something, you could be adjunct faculty to help train or teach that class. I think that would help with availability of the actual training. [Civilian]

Several OCO civilians suggested that USAF could build a cyber infrastructure that would allow offensive operators to practice in a controlled environment.

> In my brigade, they have their own infrastructure—a very limited mission, since it's new and starting up, but they have some operations out of there. They're easing into it; they're still brand new. I'm talking one to two years old. They do a lot of their planning toward that architecture, and the training is still dependent on the NSA. It's the same concepts, just working on a different computer. Some of the rules don't follow, which is nice. They have a separate set of rules. It'd be nice if the Air Force had that for themselves, or expand on the Army's architecture, which I know is not going to happen. [Civilian]

***

> One thing that would be really nice is a program so that cyber units can build their own infrastructure for training and operations. Here at NSA, the Army has taken the lead for that. They have built their own architectures to work on to do daily operations. The Air Force, we're along for the ride, and we kind of borrow time from them to do stuff. [Civilian]

Some participants pointed to a desire for the other services and entities to be able to share more of their training with USAF so that USAF can incorporate it as its own.[46]

> On the OCO side, NSA has a JCAC; it would be immensely helpful to gain access to their materials. We talk to 1N4As; we learn the same thing. But they

---

[46] A similar point was discussed in a previous section on training redundancy.

pay to have the same stuff developed; it's just in a different format, and Keesler pays for a range to be similar to the same thing that the 39th IOS [Information Operations Squadron] and JCAC has. . . . We should have access to all of that material and consolidate it so we don't have all of this redundancy and duplication of effort. We are wasting a lot of time for a lot of folks. [1B4]

## Participants Discussed KSAOs Needed Prior to Entering Training

Prior research by Hardison et al., 2019, explored USAF officer views on specific KSAOs that are needed by USAF cyber officers. In this study, we also asked enlisted and civilian participants to comment on the KSAOs that personnel should have when they are first entering their career fields.

Other sources have delved more deeply into the needed KSAOs for members of a cyber workforce, and, therefore, it was not our intent to outline the entire domain of KSAOs needed in these career fields. For example, Hardison et al., 2019, provides a review of the academic research literature describing KSAOs needed in the IT and cybersecurity fields in the private sector, and the National Initiative for Cybersecurity Education Cybersecurity Workforce Framework provides a detailed and comprehensive tool for identifying relevant KSAOs within these workforces (Newhouse et al., 2017). Instead, our goal was to determine which characteristics personnel would identify as being important for personnel to possess prior to entering the training pipeline to be successful in USAF training and, ultimately, in the USAF cyber mission.

Because of time constraints, we discussed this topic in about 80 percent of the groups.[47] Figure 7.2 shows that in a majority of discussions, someone suggested that newly arrived cyber personnel should be proactive and self-starters. In addition, in many of the groups, computer and technical skills, critical-thinking skills, the ability to learn, curiosity, and communication skills were mentioned. As we suspected, the characteristics identified were similar to those reported in Hardison et al., 2019, for officers.

---

[47] In about 20 percent of the groups, we were running low on time and excluded the question.

**Figure 7.2. Views on KSAOs Needed Prior to Entering the Cyber Training Pipeline**

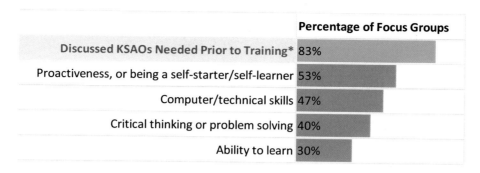

NOTE: Percentages represent the number of focus groups in which a KSAO was mentioned by at least one person. All percentages are out of a total of 30 discussions.

The following are some examples of participants' comments:

> I think that being proactive and a self-starter is a good predictive factor in determining one's success, certainly in the OCO world. Arguably on the other side as well, because there is not a well-publicized training path to achieve mastery in a lot of our units. People have to think of things on the fly and be creative. [1N4A]

***

> [The] ability to work and try things without direction is important. A lot of what you do . . . is just to keep trying things, and it can get frustrating. Some students are self-starting—they may not know what they are doing, but they will go out there and start stuff and research on their own. Others who just sit there and panic and wait to be told what to do. Being comfortable with not knowing what is going to happen or how it is going to work is a valuable attitudinal attribute to look for as well. [Workforce—other]

***

> We want an airman who says, "I like computers, I like the keyboard, I like doing these things in the IT world, and I think I can do these things for 50 years," or however [long] they want to be in the career field—let's say 20 years. [Workforce—other]

***

> The logic and problem-solving are probably the two biggest things you have to learn and understand in our career field. [1B4]

***

> Analytical thinking skills—that's a big thing. It's hard to determine someone who has that mentality—someone who can take problem sets and break them into portions to attack differently. They definitely have to come in with an open mind. [Civilian]

***

> Problem-solving and critical thinking are huge—massive—and everything challenging about the job is critical thinking and problem-solving. It's possible to

do that, but it's hard to do. There are people who have tons of experience who may pass with little critical thinking because they have so much experience, so they aren't tested on anything new, because they've experienced it all. But we need people who would be willing to learn new things to solve new problems. [1B4]

\*\*\*

Ability and will to learn. I was one of the only previous cyber personnel. It doesn't matter what your background is. [1B4]

\*\*\*

Higher IQ. Ability to take and retain enough info and synthesize. That helps. There are some who could chug away and figure out anything. But if you want to do it quickly, they are going to have to have a desire to do it. They need to be able to get a lot of info and start using it. [1B4]

Participants also offered a variety of other KSAOs beyond those shown in Figure 7.2. Those that were mentioned in 7 to 10 percent of the discussions (two or three discussions) include humility and attention to detail. The following KSAOs were mentioned in only one discussion:

- curiosity
- communication skills
- vigilance
- previous experience as an analyst
- ability to handle work/family conflict
- flexibility/adaptability
- ability to work in a team
- stress tolerance.

## Participants Offered Other Suggestions for Improvement

Participants offered a variety of other solutions not captured in the categories listed above. These solutions were mentioned less frequently than the ones discussed previously (i.e., they were mentioned in three or fewer groups), but we include them as suggestions that might nonetheless have merit:

- **Continue to develop cyber skills in those who wash out of cyber training.** Individuals who fail out of training, including some of the most advanced cyber training courses, might not be destined to become 1B4s or 1N4As, but participants conveyed that these individuals are valuable talent that USAF might still want to utilize in cyber, albeit in different roles. Participants discussed current efforts that are underway to develop individuals who wash out of initial training and mentioned that many other options exist. For instance, it would be advantageous to retain the interest and aptitude for cyber in other cyber fields that might move at a slower pace.
- **Implement self-paced training.** When asked about solutions to improve training, a few participants suggested that training be restructured to allow trainees to learn in a self-

paced environment. This included the ability to test out of content or spend additional time on topics depending on skill level.

- **Create an online forum for sharing knowledge.** Participants in a few groups discussed the potential advantages of USAF creating an online marketplace to host training and serve as a forum for the exchange of knowledge.[48] These participants explained that having an online marketplace would facilitate the exchange of ideas and advice and provide connections to training and resources that would enable airmen to stay on the cutting edge of cyber. Participants also explained that such an online marketplace would be helpful for building social networks to share information and skill sets. Beyond the more tangible technical development benefit, participants articulated the potential for culture-building and talent management on such a platform.

- **Increase accountability for maintaining proficiency.** This was mentioned in a few groups as one way to help institutionalize training requirements and ensure that resources are provided for training of the cyber workforce. That is, if continuation training and currency requirements were formalized, there would be a clearer justification for resourcing that effort. In addition, formalizing a process for evaluating the effectiveness of training would be beneficial for maintaining accountability. If no measures of how well personnel are performing in the field exist to provide feedback to training developers, then there is no formal way of demonstrating that training needs are not being met. Creating a formal process for soliciting feedback in the field on a continuing basis would be ideal because of the rapidly changing nature of cyber. It would help provide clear and systematic justification for how often training content, materials, and equipment (such as training ranges) need to be updated and the resources that need to be set aside for that purpose.

- **Eliminate obstacles that are preventing cyber work and training from being accomplished.** Eliminate "additional duties" that get in the way of training and work. Eliminate red tape by changing policy to accommodate the changing needs of cyber.[49]

- **Add more cyber training to technical schools of other career fields.** Several comments were related to personnel simply not knowing about cyber or not understanding its uses and how it relates to the work in other career fields. One participant suggested adding more cyber training to other career fields for this reason. This individual noted that it could help personnel in other career fields know when cyber might be relevant. It could also help personnel who are involved in missions to which cyberwarfare is relevant to better understand how it relates to the work that they are doing. Participants talked about how this could help USAF's mission in many ways.

- **Develop a better understanding of cyber among leadership.** Some participants expressed a general dissatisfaction with USAF leadership's understanding of cyber at all levels. Participants noted that when members of leadership do not deeply understand cyber, they have difficulty judging risk or lack of risk in making various decisions that

---

[48] This was discussed as a marketplace intended for information-sharing within USAF; however, some participants noted that more information-sharing could also be beneficial across the services.

[49] Examples include eliminating the administrative hurdles to purchasing new hardware and software; establishing official processes that would allow much more frequent updates or adjustments to training as technology changes; and eliminating the multiple decision authorities required to make changes to cyber training, the allocation of training resources, or the use of novel cyber approaches (when such approaches are low risk).

affect cyber (including decisions that affect training, technology, and tactics), and they can drastically misjudge some risks (viewing the risk as either too high or too low relative to the actual risk). They also do not necessarily understand potential gains and, therefore, might not recognize when gains outweigh risks, or vice versa. Participants explained that this misjudgment of risks and benefits can sometimes result in a lack of trust and camaraderie between leadership and subordinates. This lack of trust was mentioned as a source of burnout, issues associated with red tape, and a lack of interest in taking on nontechnical, managerial duties. In one focus group, participants expressed a desire for leadership to receive cyber training:

> We'd like to educate our leadership so that they know what we're doing, and why, and how, so that they can make decisions that facilitate that instead of limiting it—especially since a lot of people, like the general, don't [get] a clear picture of what's going on at the bottom. [SME]

***

> There's a problem with technology where there's a gap between workers and managers in what the managers know about how and why the work is being done. [SME]

***

> I think this was a problem because of the congressional mandate to fill the teams, and they just had to take whoever they could get for leadership, just like with us. Hopefully, through time, that will fix itself, and leadership will have knowledge of cyber. [SME]

***

> They just brought in a captain who is going to be a mission commander, and they went through mission training, hands on keyboard, and all that. Now they're sending him to spend time on keyboard for a little bit. Then he gets to go be a mission commander and go through leadership training. I respect that a lot more. And he has a way better idea of what to do and how to make better-informed decisions because he's been in that place—maybe not for as long, but still. [1B4]

# 8. Recommended Next Steps

The previous chapters presented many ideas and suggestions provided by the workforce to improve training. In this chapter, we present our recommendations for USAF to consider. These recommendations reflect what are the most-promising training changes from our perspective. In identifying the changes that we think are the most promising, we did not rely exclusively on the ideas offered by our participants. We considered the possibility that there could be entirely novel solutions that were not entertained by our participants. Although we considered whether any novel solutions could be relevant, all of the recommendations that we ultimately opted to suggest are grounded in comments that our participants provided. Our decisions about which options to recommend were based on our data and several other factors. These factors included, for example, the rationale behind a solution, the level of need for change, the level of positive impact that might be realized by a change, overall resource levels and cost requirements, and constraints in existing DoD policies.

We have grouped our recommendations into two categories: resource changes and structural and cultural changes. *Resource changes* are those that, if implemented, will require various degrees of human or monetary resources or will require shifting current resources around. Although the same can be said of our other category of recommendations,[50] *structural and cultural changes*, this category is less defined by resource requirements than by the scope and organizational changes that such changes will engender. Unless otherwise noted, the recommendations outlined in this chapter apply to the 1B4s, the 1N4As, and the civilian CMF workforce.

Lastly, we note that although we recommend that USAF consider the following changes to training across the lifespan, all of these options come with various trade-offs, and many would require significant resources or changes. As a result, USAF will have to carefully weigh trade-offs for each option.[51]

---

[50] The structural and cultural changes might or might not also require an outlay of resources. However, we set them apart from the resource changes because the alterations to structure or culture might require additional finesse to implement. That is, they would likely require widespread and enduring buy-in from leadership for implementing high-level and strategic changes to USAF policies and procedures. The structures and cultures involved also will not likely change as easily.

[51] Given that we have not conducted a cost-benefit analysis for these options, we cannot say which options would offer the best return on USAF's investment of time, labor, and resources.

## Resource Changes

### Develop and Proliferate More Training Simulations and Ranges

More training simulations and ranges can have a significant impact on increasing proficiency in the cyber workforce. However, care needs to be taken to make sure that the right simulations are available at the right time and to the personnel who most need them. For some purposes, for the simulations to be useful, they would need to be highly developed, complex, tailored to address specific relevant and current threats, and regularly updated. For other purposes, more-simplified simulations could be useful.

As mentioned by participants, simulations could be useful for a variety of training circumstances; more-junior personnel who are still in training could benefit from them, they could be used to help more-experienced personnel maintain currency, they could be used to test out new approaches, and they could be used to help provide training on new technology to operators already in the field. For those in the first two years of training, simulations could help facilitate better learning and could be used to get personnel on keyboard faster to help keep them engaged.

A dedicated team of airmen might be necessary to develop ranges for these purposes to ensure that the ranges are sufficiently current, appropriate for their intended use, and made available to those who need them. Because this would require additional manning, USAF would need to think critically about the feasibility of reallocating personnel from other missions or about other ways to accomplish this goal. Collaboration with the other services and gaining access to sims maintained by other organizations (e.g., NSA) could lead to significant development cost savings and better simulations overall.

Lastly, some participants noted that some useful training simulations and training ranges exist, but many airmen do not have access to them.[52] Therefore, we recommend that USAF work to remove any potential barriers to access to existing training simulations and ranges and ensure that these and any newly developed ranges be made widely available.

### Find New Ways to Test Cyber Capabilities Using Live Red Forces, but Do So Selectively

Using live red forces and capture-the-flag exercises to test cyber capabilities would be beneficial for training and morale if they are well designed, with cyber workforce training and

---

[52] Although multiple participants identified access to the simulations as an issue, we did not follow up to find out what was resulting in the access issues. Potential elements inhibiting access could be purely administrative (e.g., individual supervisors might not want personnel to be spending their time engaged in those activities, or there might be policies limiting the numbers of personnel that can participate in simulations), or there might be technology or logistics constraints (e.g., number of portals, licenses, bandwidth, security clearances, network limitations, funding, or even policies forbidding specific connectivity). Therefore, we recommend further exploration of the core issues driving limited access to help understand how best to remedy the access issue.

development (i.e., development of cyber technical skills and tactics) in mind. Participants acknowledged that, because constraints have to be placed on cyber play within some exercises, the exercises do not necessarily simulate adversary behavior during real missions and might limit the benefits. Because of the planning and expense associated with these events, thought would need to be given to how often such exercises would be useful and for whom. Ideally, all personnel would be able to participate in such exercises regularly.

## Institute Cyber Aptitude Screening

To make the best use of training resources, USAF needs to make sure that it is bringing in the right talent prior to sending personnel to training. Although we are aware that USAF has a variety of studies underway to identify predictors of cyber success, to our knowledge, no validated test of cyber aptitude is currently being administered or used for selection in the 1B4 career field.

The 1N4As have been using an ASVAB cyber subtest for screening their incoming personnel; however, this cyber subtest focuses on assessing *existing cyber knowledge*. It does not assess someone's *potential cyber aptitude* independent of the person's prior acquired knowledge and skills.[53] The 1N4As have also been screened using a new selection model that combines scores from the Tailored Adaptive Personality Assessment (TAPAS) and two ASVAB General Science and Math Knowledge subtests.[54] Anecdotal evidence suggests that these new 1N4A TAPAS and ASVAB screening requirements are seen as beneficial in predicting training success. As one 1N4 SME explained,

---

[53] 1N4As are required to have either a minimum score of 62 (out of 100) on USAF's general aptitude ASVAB composite or a minimum score of 57 (out of 100) on the general aptitude composite and a minimum score of 60 on the ASVAB Cyber Test (CT) (Air Force Personnel Center, 2019, Attachment 4). The CT, previously known as the Information/Communications Technology Literacy Test, includes content assessing existing knowledge of cyber (Morris and Waage, 2012) and, therefore, might not be as useful at identifying potential in personnel who do not have any prior cyber experience. For more information about the CT, see Trippe et al., 2014. For more discussion of some types of cyber tests that could be considered for USAF selection purposes, see Morris and Waage, 2012.

[54] TAPAS is a personality assessment tool that has been administered to military applicants for several years. According to the career-field manager, the 1N4A career field uses the TAPAS subtest that assesses "tolerance" to screen personnel. This subtest is designed to measure whether "individuals are interested in other cultures and opinions that may differ from their own" and whether "they are willing to adapt to novel environments and situations" (Nye et al., 2012, p. 6). TAPAS is combined with a set of ASVAB subtests modeled after the Navy's cyber screening formula. The career-field manager explained that

> Utilization of Tailored Personality Assessment System and the two-factor Armed Services Vocational Aptitude Battery subtest (General Science [GS] and Math Knowledge [MK]) model score was implemented for entry into the 1N4X1A specialty as of 1 October 2019. . . . We accept members at the AT46 qualifying score, which means they are at the 56th percentile or above the proposed ASVAB and TAPAS composite. Our interest in arithmetic and math knowledge scores stems from the Navy having higher pass rates at JCAC by increasing their scores. The Navy model utilizes AR [arithmetic reasoning]+2*MK+GS. . . . [Our] model was created by AFPC/DSYX [Air Force Personnel Center, Strategic Research and Assessment Branch] and AF/A1 (Dr. Katie Gunther and team).

[There has been] positive feedback from both 1N4A schools (Goodfellow AFB and [Naval Air Station Pensacola] Corry Station) regarding the positive changes we have seen utilizing the new model (general belief that students are [of a] more appropriate caliber). . . . In [fiscal year] FY 19, the Air Force overall attrition dropped below 20 percent for the first time. . . . Our overall attrition dropped from 27.3 percent during FY 18 to 14.6 percent during FY 19. [1N4]

Other assessments exist that also might be useful in assessing cyber *potential*, but they are not currently in use in any of these career fields. For example, the University of Maryland's Applied Research Laboratory for Intelligence and Security—formerly the Center for Advanced Study of Language—has been developing the Cyber Aptitude and Talent Assessment for USAF.

To develop and validate a test that is designed specifically to predict cyber aptitude or cyber potential, predictive validity studies are needed (in which performance of cyber personnel in training or on the job is measured and correlated with scores on a variety of potential cyber screening tests). This can help decisionmakers identify which tests are the best predictors and whether a series of tests is useful. Care should be taken to ensure that such a screening tool or set of tools does not focus too much on prior knowledge of cyber when no such cyber experience is needed. That is, if knowledge of cyber is used as a proxy for aptitude, it might tend to exclude key groups of interest who would be successful but who might be currently underrepresented in the career field (e.g., women, minorities, creative thinkers who might be good problem-solvers but lack a technical background).[55]

### Create an Online Forum for Learning, Information-Sharing, and Talent Management

We learned from participants that forums have been created where training knowledge and information are shared but that those forums were developed informally and, therefore, are not necessarily known or widely utilized across the career field. However, building such a forum—one that was developed and supported formally and utilized widely—would be a fairly inexpensive way of sharing access to information and training within the career field. It could be designed to accommodate access to just-in-time training if needed and also used to make training individualized, more tailored, and more accessible across the force. A centralized forum could be used to provide immediate feedback to training course developers about the effectiveness of existing training and to identify gaps in skill sets that commanders need.

The forum could also be used to help address some concerns that participants expressed about utilization of talent. It could be designed to help support talent management by showing what certifications and experience members of the workforce have. It could also be designed to help leaders identify personnel who have the skill sets that align with a particular assignment. Because some information is likely to be classified (e.g., experience and skills gained through

---

[55] For more on how to validate and evaluate the fairness of such a test, see the *Standards for Educational and Psychological Testing* (American Educational Research Association, American Psychological Association, and National Council on Measurement in Education, 2014) and the *Principles for the Validation and Use of Personnel Selection Procedures* (Society for Industrial and Organizational Psychology, 2003).

particular assignments, such as NSA), it is possible that both classified and unclassified forums could be useful.

If such a forum were developed, however, care should be taken to make it as useful as possible and avoid some circumstances that could render it useless or defunct. For example, the forum was discussed as a marketplace intended for information-sharing within USAF, but some participants noted that more information-sharing could also be beneficial across the services. It is certainly possible that information-sharing within USAF alone could be beneficial; however, there might be limits to the forum's usefulness if it cannot also foster information-sharing and lessons learned in and with the other services. In addition, there might be lessons to be learned from other information-sharing forums, such as the Army Knowledge Online portal or the evolution of the Air Force Knowledge Now portal, that might be important for ensuring that the forum is, in fact, useful to the cyber community and that its usefulness and original intent are maintained over time.

## *Provide More Structure and Oversight of Trainings Developed by Individual Units*

We heard from participants that unit-created trainings are mostly informal and lack guidelines for establishing consistent standards in training quality and topics. Because these trainings are normally led by operators with specific knowledge, motivations, and teaching abilities, if these operators leave the unit, their trainings leave with them. To alleviate this problem, USAF could take steps to develop guidance to formalize the trainings more, add structure, and help units properly resource the trainings. USAF could also provide ongoing oversight for existing unit trainings.

Although training standards should be consistent among all units, some units might have different resources, missions, and other idiosyncrasies that affect training. When implementing guidance or oversight, USAF should account for these differences by allowing some flexibility with how such training is administered or modified to fit the unit.[56] Although the skills and abilities of the operators should be consistent, certain topics might be more or less relevant for certain units. Additionally, while some units might be happy to provide training, others expressed frustration with the need to have additional training for the operators and with the associated resources that would be required. Some participants said they felt that the training was only necessary because IST was insufficient and that there was a lack of opportunities for continuation training. These units might be hesitant to support training without additional resources, such as funding, instructors, and other training materials, such as simulation ranges.[57]

---

[56] Although flexibility would be the goal, rules and boundaries would need to be established by clear policy and enforced.

[57] If training requirements are passed on to individual follow-on units instead of being better addressed at the IST level, those insufficiencies in training need to be acknowledged and addressed formally and funded through officially designated resources and training time at the units.

## Structural and Cultural Changes

### Redesign Training to Be Flexible and Responsive to Just-In-Time Needs and Tailored to Airmen's Existing Capabilities

Although the cyber training pipeline provides opportunities for continuation training and relevant courses for work, operators commented that these courses were often redundant or irrelevant to their positions, did not take into account prior training and experience (particularly in IST), and used outdated teaching materials or course materials that were not suited for their roles. To remedy these situations, the training pipeline could be redesigned to provide training that better supports the needs of the cyber workforce. Training needs differ by assignment, and the technology changes over time, so training can become outdated quickly. Moreover, participants expressed an interest in being able to go back and retake coursework that might have changed since they initially took it and being able to take training specific to their assignment or a particular mission, when the need arises. Both circumstances suggest that there is an appetite for just-in-time training by making a wide variety of trainings and training resources (including even materials from IST) widely accessible so that personnel in the field can access them as needed.[58]

In addition, flexibility in the coursework that operators need to complete could better account for operators' existing KSAs in cyber. Although testing out certainly would be one step that might help address this flexibility, tailoring could be more sophisticated; pretesting or other forms of screening could be used to determine someone's skill levels throughout training (including prior to entering a course or a course block and in determining what continuation or currency training an individual needs most), and, depending on the results of that test or screening, the course depth, length, and even content could be tailored to that individual's need.

With these changes to the training pipeline, USAF might be able to save resources used and possibly reduce the time needed to complete some trainings. The saved resources could be used to expand the topics covered in continuation trainings, increase the number of courses available, and update the teaching materials. Operators would be able to learn more information and information that would be more relevant to their roles. However, it is also worth noting that accelerated and tailored training could create undesirable "breaks in training" during which an individual is waiting for a slot to open in the next level of training in the pipeline. Impacts on end-to-end training pipeline flow would need to be further explored.

---

[58] Note that some just-in-time training does exist and occurs regularly in certain circumstances in USAF. (Some personnel are sent to special training here and there as a matter of course, and deployment trainings and mission-specific or unit-specific trainings could be offered as some examples of just-in-time training that are used commonly in many career fields.) However, we are not aware of any USAF career fields (officer or enlisted) that have institutionalized just-in-time training or tailored training as a formal approach to training across the lifespan in the career field. Instead, the enlisted career fields all operate primarily on the 3/5/7/9-level upgrade system that suggests that certain types of training are needed at certain points in one's career—and needed by everyone at that point in their career. For more on the 3/5/7/9-level upgrade system in general, see Air Force Instruction 36-2101, 2017.

Lastly, such flexible training might mean that the training would be much shorter for some individuals than for others. Individuals for whom the training is shorter would have less exposure to USAF rules, procedures, and culture. As a result, impacts of such a flexible training timeline on USAF's ability to indoctrinate personnel to USAF culture, rules, and procedures would need to be considered.

## Create Senior Technical Roles That Are Not Management Oriented

Participants talked about the need to find a way to keep personnel on keyboard, both to help maintain proficiency and to help address retention issues (see Volume II for more on the retention piece) by allowing personnel to continue to do the work they love most,[59] and this applied to both civilians and enlisted personnel. Many participants noted that a warrant officer program for enlisted airmen would address this but pointed out that USAF has no such program currently. Although participants acknowledged that a warrant officer program might never be a possibility within USAF, many mentioned the benefits of having such a program.

Some noted that there could be ways to achieve the benefits that make a warrant officer program so attractive, specifically the ability to continually increase someone's pay but still allow them to remain on keyboard without requiring them to take on a leadership role. Finding a way to allow this ability for both civilians and enlisted personnel would be ideal.[60]

As one example, a few participants mentioned that the Cyber Excepted Service will allow civilian members to receive merit-based pay increases without moving up in pay grade. If this option is offered to civilian cyber personnel widely, and if a similar program could be developed to address the same issue with enlisted personnel, it might prevent some of the issues that participants raised, including enlisted attempts to prevent promotion by intentionally failing Weighted Airman Promotion System tests or high-performing civilians and enlisted personnel being tempted to leave the service so that they can continue to spend time on keyboard.

## Better Education for the Entire USAF About What the Cyber Workforce Does and How That Work Fits into the Bigger Mission

As noted earlier, there was a clear perception among members of the workforce that cyber personnel are often misutilized, and participants noted that this misutilization starts at the recruiting stage and goes all the way up to assignment decisions at later stages in one's career. Notably, a career-field manager echoed these sentiments, explaining how arbitrary lines that delineate cyber AFSCs result in a misconception about which AFSC is able to perform which

---

[59] This recommendation is discussed in both Volume I and Volume II of this report because it was discussed by participants as being relevant both to maintenance of the workforce's technical skills and to reasons personnel might decide to separate from USAF.

[60] This issue was raised in prior research that looked at cyber officers (Hardison et al., 2019), and other career fields have also explored this issue. For example, a recent report explored the idea of instituting both a warrant officer program and a technical track for pilots (Robbert et al., 2018).

role,[61] and some individuals view cyber AFSCs as interchangeable. This lack of understanding regarding performance capabilities of these AFSCs can be problematic. For example, a highly skilled airman could be misutilized if there is not clarity on the person's capabilities, and this misutilization could be detrimental (or a missed opportunity) to overall mission success.

Our participants explained that this overall lack of understanding of cyber affects cyber training in several ways. For example, some participants noted that cyber training needs to be different from that of most other AFSCs because of the constant and rapidly changing nature of the work. They also noted that personnel who make resource decisions about cyber often do not have cyber expertise, and that can lead to decisions about how to manage and resource training that fail to take into consideration the uniqueness of cyber. In addition, participants talked about personnel utilization problems in which personnel's skill sets are not being fully utilized in some assignments. It is also possible that, for cyber personnel, the inclusion of additional duties on a daily basis might be more disruptive to their ability to execute the mission and develop an appropriate depth of skill than it is in other career fields. That is, cyber activities might require many hours of concentration that, when disrupted, prevent someone from being able to follow through on some activity that they have started. For this reason, rethinking how additional duties are allocated to personnel in different career fields might be warranted. However, those who have decisionmaking power over how much burden each career field shoulders with respect to additional duties would need to better understand the nature of cyber work. These are just a few examples of why better USAF-wide understanding of cyber might be beneficial.

*Hire and Retain Experienced Instructors*

A major training challenge discussed by cyber operators was the presence of ineffective instructors in both initial and continuation trainings. Instructors were often criticized for being poor teachers and for having a general lack of experience. This suggests that instructors might need better preparation for teaching.[62] It also suggests that greater care in selecting instructors with prior on-the-job experience is important. As some participants suggested, an influx of experienced instructors (i.e., instructors who come equipped with extensive on-the-job military cyber experience) would help cyber operators be more prepared for their roles because the operators would be able to learn from others who have been placed in similar situations. This issue was particularly relevant for offensive cyber operators, who often said that most educators

---

[61] Note that, at the time this study was conducted, USAF was in the process of considering a merger of the 1N4A and 1B4 career fields because of the significant overlap in the training, skill sets, and work performed by these two groups.

[62] This includes potentially improving the train-the-trainer courses, finding better ways to screen instructors to identify personnel who have an aptitude for teaching and mentoring others, and putting forth additional resources to support instructor development in other ways (e.g., the development of new training programs for instructors and sending instructors to specialized technical cyber courses to further develop their depth of technical expertise in key areas). Further research should explore the efficacy and benefits of these types of improvements to instructor selection and training programs.

came from a defensive background. Their lack of offensive experience was noted by several participants who said that training effectiveness was severely hampered by the instructors' inexperience. Some participants suggested having experienced operators serve as adjunct faculty, which could be a way of using their expertise and potentially keeping them more connected to the more junior cyber workforce. An increase in experienced instructors could lead to more training sessions being made available, reduce washout rates, and improve training effectiveness.

# Appendix A. Additional Information About the Focus Groups and the Questionnaire

## Discussion Participants and Topics of Discussion

The research team conducted a total of 25 in-person discussions and five phone interviews with the 1B4s, 1N4As, and CMF civilians. In seven of the in-person discussions, only one person volunteered, meaning that those discussions functioned as an interview instead of a focus group. The five phone discussions were all held as interviews with one participant per discussion. Across all of these discussions, the number of participants ranged from three to seven, and there was an average of 2.5 participants per group. Focus groups lasted an hour and a half and covered both training issues (discussed in this volume) and recruiting and retention issues (discussed in Volume II). The primary questions that we asked on recruiting and retention were as follows:[63]

- Do you think there is a problem attracting (enlisted or civilian) cyber personnel to join USAF's cyber workforce? Why or why not?
- Do you think there is a problem retaining (enlisted or civilian) cyber personnel in USAF's cyber workforce?

The primary questions that we asked on training were as follows:

- Are there gaps in your cyber community's KSAOs that are not being adequately addressed in training?
- Do you think training and development in the cyber community needs to be improved? If so, why? How?
- Are there any obstacles preventing the cyber community from being well trained or developed?
- Is there technology or equipment that you need for training that you don't have access to or that doesn't exist?
- What are the KSAOs people need to bring to the training pipeline?

## Coding the Qualitative Comments from Our Discussions

To analyze the data collected from our discussions with members of the cyber workforce, we identified and sorted excerpts from the discussion transcripts based on relevant topics or

---

[63] These questions were asked in the order presented here, unless a question was spontaneously addressed by participants before we reached that point in our protocol. For the most part, the discussion topics generally proceeded in the order presented here.

themes.[64] By coding participants' comments in this way, we were able to quantify the frequency with which particular themes were mentioned across all of the discussions and identify relevant quotations that exemplified each theme.

To estimate the level of agreement between coders, we double-coded four focus group transcripts. We used this information to calculate two agreement ratios. The first ratio is a more lenient estimate of agreement between coders, and the second is more conservative. For the more lenient agreement ratio, we considered agreement as having occurred in two ways: either both coders coded a topic as being mentioned, or both did not code a topic as being mentioned. We then counted the number of times in each transcript that the raters' codes agreed in this way and divided that number by the total number of codes in our coding list (85 codes). Doing this gave us an overall percentage agreement for each transcript. Averaging these ratios across the four transcripts, we got an inter-coder agreement ratio of 0.89.

To estimate agreement more conservatively, we focused only on codes that were applied to a given discussion by at least one coder. That is, we divided the number of codes agreed upon by both coders in a given transcript by the total number of codes applied to that transcript by at least one coder. Averaging these ratios across the four transcripts, we got an average inter-coder agreement ratio of 0.76.[65]

## Questionnaire Participants

In the focus group discussions with members of the workforce, a questionnaire was administered.[66] The questionnaire consisted of a series of Likert-scale questions (e.g., on a scale of 1 to 5). For example, one question asked participants to evaluate how valuable certain training features (e.g., live red forces) would be to implement. Other Likert-scale items provided a statement, such as, "My training prepared me for the responsibilities of my specialty," and respondents had to rate the extent to which they agreed or disagreed.

In addition to the Likert-scale questions, participants were given two open-ended questions to which they were asked to provide written responses:

- If you could redesign the training for cyber professionals in your workforce community (IST, continuation training, availability of training courses, access to resources, timeliness of training, or any other aspects), what changes would you make? How would it be different from the existing cyber training?

---

[64] We allowed the content of the discussion transcripts and our initial impressions and memory of the frequently mentioned comments to drive the initial set of themes. That is, we used a purely inductive approach based on participant responses. We did not attempt to identify themes before we held the discussions.

[65] There is no single agreed-upon approach for evaluating agreement of coding. In addition, there is no single agreed-upon level of agreement that is considered acceptable. However, for exploratory research studies, the levels of agreement might not need to be as stringent: 0.70, 0.80, and 0.90 are among the levels of agreement that are commonly listed as acceptable.

[66] Much of this section also appears in Hardison et al., 2021.

- Please provide any additional comments here.

Finally, participants were asked to provide basic demographic information about their rank and pay grade, job type, and training background. As shown in Table A.1, a total of 67 participants completed a questionnaire,[67] although some participants left questions blank. Notably, only seven participants were civilians. Thus, mean scores should be interpreted with caution because the scores garnered from the small sample of respondents might not generalize to all civilians.

**Table A.1. Number of Participants Who Responded to the Questionnaire**

| Type of Discussion | Sample Size |
|---|---|
| By specialty | |
| 1B4 | 40 |
| 1N4A | 20 |
| CMF civilian | 7 |
| By base | |
| Fort Meade | 40 |
| JBSA | 12 |
| Scott Air Force Base | 15 |
| By self-reported work role | |
| DCO | 27 |
| OCO | 25 |
| Both OCO and DCO | 9 |
| Other (e.g., staff, finances, intel support) or unknown (e.g., not OCO/DCO) | 6 |

Although participants were asked to attend a group for either OCO or DCO participants, depending on their work roles, we also asked participants to report their work roles on the questionnaire. As shown in the table, that resulted in a different count for OCO and DCO representation than what we report for the focus group results. For example, some participants reported that their work contains both OCO and DCO roles, and many reported having another role as well. The "other" category includes written-in responses by the participants and includes the following: "tech school," "intel support to national mission," "malware analysis," "finances," "not OCO/DCO," and "I have no expertise."

---

[67] The number of surveys completed is smaller than the number of discussion participants because those who participated by phone were not administered a questionnaire. All of the participants who attended in person completed a questionnaire.

# Appendix B. Questionnaire Write-In Responses About Ways to Improve Training

On the questionnaire, we asked participants two open-ended questions that resulted in responses related to training. The first question was, "How would you improve training?" We grouped participants' written responses to this question into 14 categories and an additional category ("other") created to capture all of the other responses (see Table B.1). As shown in the table, the topics and comments are, in many cases, similar to those discussed in the main body of the report.

Our second question asked whether participants had any additional comments, and many participants wrote in responses to that question as well. Some duplicated information discussed in detail elsewhere in the report. Responses that provide additional insights are shown in Table B.2.

**Table B.1. Open-Ended Question Results: How Would You Improve Training?**

| Category | Number of Mentions[c] | Sample Responses |
|---|---|---|
| Make broad training improvements, such as changing content or delivery method | 20 | • The pace of the training which I feel is a little too fast for people cross-training from non-cyber careers<br>• Courses in general needed to be highly adaptable and integrate the latest information as much as possible<br>• Training should be 12+ months via PCS and be highly demanding<br>• With the training content being out of date compared to the public sector and an expedited training pipeline, training graduates are not prepared to adequately handle the cyber environment<br>• Online module-based training<br>• Make training more self-paced to get people out to mission faster<br>• 1N4A do not need the additional training in 1N4B school<br>• There needs to be more of an incentive to take on instructor duty (pay/assignment)<br>• Time between attending training and doing a job is too much. Skills become lost.<br>• Removal of repetitive and non-applicable training which results in wasted time/money/personnel<br>• Allow the trainee to pick 2–4 electives that are aligned with their interests<br>• Training should be hands on focused and required annually<br>• Add a course for operationally focused intel for cyber taught by EAs/operators; Get our operators and EAs with real world hacking tools<br>• EAs are limited by availability of CYBER3800 |

| Category | Number of Mentions[c] | Sample Responses |
|---|---|---|
| Make improvements specific to mission qualification training, continuation training, or both | 14 | • Continuation training SANS courses: Windows Forensics, Memory Forensics, Network Forensics, Forensics Analysts, etc.<br>• I genuinely feel like there is no system in place to "train" operators for the mission set we are tested with—threat hunting.<br>• I would use a combination of skills gathered from initial training against a sim environment (Red Team or Emulation Cell) to further expand the experience based on the mission set<br>• Continuation training needs to be constant<br>• Continuation and on the job training need to be revamped and in some cases created because it is not adequate to prepare personnel outside of mission windows; Continuation training is almost nonexistent for some positions<br>• Multiple members in my unit, 1N4As, feel as if all their Air Force centric training related to cyber stopped at JCAC<br>• There is no 5/7 level skill upgrade training.<br>• My main concern with training is that it is not a regular priority after the member has been assigned to an operational unit. |
| Implement practice environments | 12 | • Training on the range—lots of this<br>• Procure simulators and training ranges or take advantages of ranges across the DoD.<br>• Specifically head to head training between offensive and defensive teams, and training ranges with enough resources to handle a whole team operating on it simultaneously<br>• Ready access to SIM; Red on blue training with balance of book and hands on training<br>• Ensure that all airmen get keyboard time in courses, rather than learning from a book or slides<br>• The lack of adequate training networks at units, personnel have to learn how to use the mission tools while on mission meaning resources are not being focused solely on the mission.<br>• More Netwars/Capture the Flag type events, the open nature encourages self-study/advancement similar to on the job activities<br>• More real-world exercises where we can practice tradecraft |
| Tailor training to work roles | 10 | • Have specialized courses that focus on what your actual job will be. I did go through CWO but that was not really focused on what I will be doing, it was still more a general course<br>• Start to get proficiencies of students (host or network) and have them become experts on that subject.<br>• Specialized training is needed—network forensics—disk etc. However, our specialization needs to be matched better with our jobs.<br>• Ideally, we would have tailored for each member based on their projected assignment, so we can get fully trained into the fight faster.<br>• Each individual needs to be trained specifically for their career path and teams need to train like they're on a mission.<br>• Train to a more specific position instead of the shotgun/jack of all trades training we receive now.<br>• Pick one focus offense/defense/malware/forensics and create a bunch of shreds not one AFSC for all |

| Category | Number of Mentions[c] | Sample Responses |
|---|---|---|
| Make improvements specific to IST | 7 | • Initial skills training needs to be expanded a bit, but is a good foundation<br>• UCT did not focus enough on the "why" when it came to technical training. It got too far in the woods with obscure policy, and not with technical competency<br>• The AETC model for training does not allow for on the spot corrections/updates. This leaves to an initial skills training that is outdated and filled with useless information<br>• It also felt like some of the concepts in CWO/tech school, the topics that needed to be expanded upon with additional information were not allowed due to meeting course length restrictions<br>• JCAC does NOT prepare airmen for RIOT (CNOQC) which is the baseline requirement for ALL other services[a] |
| Implement skill assessment or performance tracking | 6 | • If you already have the knowledge to test out, like IT fundamentals, that course was a complete waste of time.<br>• There should also be some kind of assessment to ensure training is maintaining desired skills/knowledge<br>• Airmen should go to JCAC then CWO, then to a place where they are trained on a specific job role/given a JQS/JQR [job qualification standard/job qualification requirement]<br>• Allow credit for NETA pre-req with JCAC completion or test out option<br>• Include a regular continuation training program that requires updating/revalidation of skills |
| Offer more non-USAF training options | 3 | • Commercial courses are usually the best sources, or those provided by academic institutions<br>• 1B4s need to be enrolled in collegiate level cyber security and computer science courses. Industry standard courses already exist (i.e., SANS, GCIA [GIAC Certified Intrusion Analyst]) and should be the minimum standard<br>• Leadership needs to be more aware of the benefits of industry training and public sector conference |
| USAF should own more training | 3 | • Have the Air Force own all training<br>• We are really focused on RIOT as premier cyber training, but its owned by the NSA. We have limited ability to shape or control content and training at times only indirectly benefits non-agency mission<br>• Atrophy of skills is real and development upon new accessions to our unit relies almost solely on contractors/industry |
| Raise the bar in training | 3 | • Increase the standards of training<br>• DCO should have stricter entry conditions with a higher washout rate<br>• Current training has the bar set too low. I feel we allowed anyone to pass to up our numbers |
| Incorporate both OCO and DCO coursework | 2 | • Right now training is split between OCO and DCO. I believe that every 1B4 should be trained the same<br>• DCO should get partial training in OCO pipeline |
| Identify appropriate personnel | 2 | • Hire the right category—computer science, cyber security majors<br>• Allow better cross-training options |
| Develop cyber career training pipeline | 2 | • Build cyber career paths across the board; Build a training pipeline that's not incomplete; i.e., one that provides cyber weapon system operators with the skill set of knowledge, skills, and abilities required to perform operational duties<br>• There should be well defined paths with milestones set to mark knowledge and performance levels |
| Increase pay[b] | 2 | • Increase in civilian pay grades for retention purposes<br>• Increase pay—peers leaving the workforce for $150K is tempting |

97

| Category | Number of Mentions[c] | Sample Responses |
|---|---|---|
| Do not change training | 2 | <ul><li>I would not make changes to the current training</li><li>I would not change anything</li></ul> |
| Other | 15 | <ul><li>Stand up more FTU [formal training units]; Take training burden off of units</li><li>I think its already well on its way to getting better on its own.</li><li>The Air Force should consider creating a training pipeline for OCO; Move schoolhouse out of AETC</li><li>Real actual training for all skill levels; Acknowledge that failure is okay and don't avoid it.</li><li>If someone is placed in a unit that is not primarily supporting cyber, that member is not afforded or informed of training opportunities</li><li>Incorporate cyber schools for offensive/defensive tracks</li><li>Remove UGT [upgrade training] 3/5/7 skill-level tasks</li><li>Make it so that 1B4s cannot have staff positions (. . . training managers, security managers, etc.) until they have gone through the training pipeline</li><li>Make unclassified classes available to yellow badge AMN [airmen]; open seats to everyone if available even in "private" classes</li><li>Dedicated teams towards engineering and development at local units, and all levels of training</li><li>Initial skills training/CBTs [computer-based trainings] should be available and encouraged beyond cross-train eligible individuals outside of "specific" career fields</li><li>Study in strategic policy for cyber and operational policy for cyber executive seminar/working group; Allow E6-E9, GG13+, D3+ to have visibility on cyber policy transition impacting their work centers</li><li>JCAC into a follow-on school that blends 1B4 operations skills (on keys) with 1N4A intelligence fundamentals (IC [intelligence community] requirements process, analysis, reporting, briefing)</li><li>1N4X1As should be the designated AFSC for the ION [interactive on-net]work role at the agency</li><li>It's not the training, it's the ability to USE the training</li></ul> |

NOTES: Eleven of the participants (of 67 total questionnaire participants) did not respond to this question.
[a] A review of the JCAC curriculum is conducted every two years, and each service has a vote on changes or modifications. This is done through a CTAG board. The CTAG report results in changes to the course. JCAC was revamped in 2015, and, according to our SME, the course after that change was vastly different from how it was prior to the change. It is not clear whether this participant's comment refers to JCAC before or after that revision.
[b] This issue of increased pay is included for completeness of the results table. However, it is also relevant to our Volume II work and, therefore, is referenced in that report as well.
[c] Out of 56 participants.

**Table B.2. Open-Ended Question Results: Provide Additional Comments Here**

| Category | Sample Responses |
|---|---|
| Cyber wartime policy impacting morale | • Policy issues appear to be a critical issue for cyber mission success. In the event of cyber hostilities during wartime, I am fearful our policy for cyber will have the US at a military disadvantage. Wartime cyber policy contingencies are critical to US security during wartime, but will likely be too late. This is impacting workforce morale. These are small people who know whether they are successful or not; and they may need a vision to show them where they fit into the larger cyber strategy to retain them. |
| Additional duties and work structure | • Two other things get in the way of properly training cyber personnel, additional duties and the rank structure. The Air Force does not allow personnel to properly focus on learning their job skills due to distractions involving additional duties or they get pulled away from technical work to do admin work at the SNCO level. Personally, I know members who have purposely worked to not promote for fear of not being allowed to be technical. The removal of personnel from technical to admin also applied to the officer side as well, personnel starting around captain tend to be pulled away from the technical side. Because of the rigid rank structure and required additional duties, we are putting ourselves in a bad position for enhancing and building our skills to our adversaries. |
| Utilizing personnel | • Those with cyber skills/training/qualifications should be able to have options where to work to professionally develop and impact their work center. Aka if a 1N4B is placed in a cyber billet, there is a good chance it will be less useful than someone who chose to work cyber or completed JCAC.<br>• Talent management is so incredibly important to the success of any training pipeline. It enables real world experience tied to the training while allowing true progression<br>• An effort must be made to consolidate cyber work roles under the same squadron or group and to not deviate from that model. If this is not done, skills will continue to atrophy for those separated from the vast majority of the workforce. |
| Pay and warrant officers[a] | • 1B4s lost [because] many good operators and analysts [are] chasing money and opportunities to stay technical/warrant officers are needed bad.<br>• The current mentality of Air Force leadership on bonuses/pay for enlisted operators will result in further retention problems of fully certified operators; other branches are offering greater pay incentives to retain their members. |
| FTU | • When it comes to other roles that are not specialized in cyber (1N3s, 1N0s, 1N4Bs) an FTU or initial training format would help with overall mission capacity. |
| Training | • Offer cyber training to all AFSCs related to cyber not just 1N4A & 1B4s<br>• Publish guidance and hold everyone accountable; training is serious business. Institutionalize crew progression and operations career path and work with MAJCOM, Air Force, and AETC to get there. **Not** "out of hide"; take away from maintaining Mission Ready (MR) status. Lastly, units need to correctly identify training requirements and [have] HHQ [higher headquarters] help to ensure requirements are accurate and achievable. |

[a] This issue of increased pay is included for completeness of the results table. However, it is relevant to our Volume II work and, therefore, is referenced in that report as well.

# Appendix C. Other Comments from the Focus Group Discussions and the Questionnaire

This appendix contains a summary of other comment topics discussed by our participants that were not covered elsewhere in the report. These comment topics are of two types.

The first type reflects responses that resulted from us asking direct questions at the end of the discussion, when time permitted, about specific aspects of training. These topics differ from those presented in the main chapters of the report in that these topics were not conversations that came up organically in response to our broad questions about what participants thought needed to be improved in training and how they would change training. These topics were instead prompted by questions about washout rates, the mentor/mentee model, whether training should focus on developing technical skills only or something else, and whether training should focus more on developing narrow tasks or on teaching the entire end-to-end mission.

The second type is the topics that were raised by our participants organically, in response to our broad training questions, but that did not directly relate to the question of improving training. These topics include pay equity issues, which we discuss in Volume II of this report, and the possibility of a merger between the 1N4As and 1B4s, which we discuss later in this appendix.

## Thoughts on Washout Rates

During the discussion, we talked about washout rates and asked participants whether they felt that the washout rates were too high.[68] Figure C.1 summarizes participant responses. Of the participants who directly answered the question, most believed that the washout rates were acceptable, and some even felt that the bar for training should be higher. A few participants thought that it should be lower.

---

[68] It is worth noting that most participants likely do not know the most-current washout rates for various courses; however, they would have a sense for them based on the reputation of the courses, conversations that occur within the career field about the difficulty of certain courses, and their own experiences in the courses.

**Figure C.1. Views on Washout Rates**

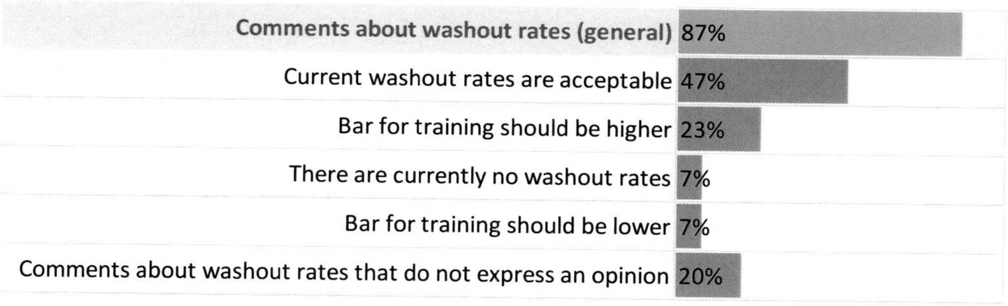

| | |
|---|---|
| Comments about washout rates (general) | 87% |
| Current washout rates are acceptable | 47% |
| Bar for training should be higher | 23% |
| There are currently no washout rates | 7% |
| Bar for training should be lower | 7% |
| Comments about washout rates that do not express an opinion | 20% |

NOTE: No opposite sentiment was offered. Percentages represent the number of focus groups in which a topic was mentioned by at least one person. All percentages are out of a total of 30 discussions.

Other comments that were offered in response to this question included the following:

- "They need better screening prior to sending people to training."
- "New airmen are more likely to wash out than experienced ones."
- "JCAC is good at filtering people out."
- "College graduates fare better in training than high school graduates."
- "The criteria for determining who washes out and who stays should be improved."
- "Training is more focused on weeding out people than teaching them."
- "Washout rates are high because people are not prepared for the difficulty of training."

# Views on the Specific Goals for and Approaches to Training in the Cyber Workforce

In most discussions, we asked participants several specific questions about possible approaches to training. Figure C.2 summarizes participant responses.

**Figure C.2. Views on Specific Goals for and Approaches to Training**

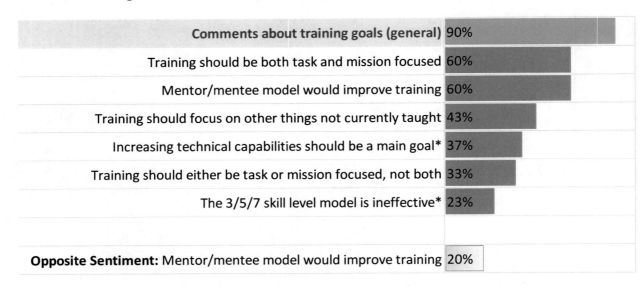

| | |
|---|---|
| Comments about training goals (general) | 90% |
| Training should be both task and mission focused | 60% |
| Mentor/mentee model would improve training | 60% |
| Training should focus on other things not currently taught | 43% |
| Increasing technical capabilities should be a main goal* | 37% |
| Training should either be task or mission focused, not both | 33% |
| The 3/5/7 skill level model is ineffective* | 23% |
| **Opposite Sentiment:** Mentor/mentee model would improve training | 20% |

NOTE: Sometimes, a view was raised by one person, and an opposite view was expressed by someone in the same discussion group. In those cases, the same discussion would be counted in both the topic frequency and the opposite sentiment frequency. For some topics, no opposite sentiment was expressed in the workforce discussions. Where an opposite sentiment was expressed in 3 to 7 percent of the workforce focus groups (i.e., one or two groups), the view is marked with an asterisk. Percentages represent the number of focus groups in which a view was mentioned by at least one person. All percentages are out of a total of 30 discussions.

The first question asked whether training should be focused on narrow tasks or whether it is more important to focus on the end-to-end mission (e.g., intel, finding access, developing a tool, monitoring). In the majority of discussions, the response to this question was "both." But, in some discussions, the other two views were also expressed, and both of these views were expressed with about the same frequency. In the cases in which participants argued for one over the other, their comments supported the conclusion that there is a time and a place for focusing on either aspect of training. In the comments in which participants said both are needed, they talked about how the failure to include either one could lead to gaps in the workforce's understanding. Some participants expressed the view that USAF needs to focus on incorporating the bigger picture more than it currently does.

In addition, in some discussions, we asked whether a mentor/mentee model, in which personnel take time and are available to help train, develop, and mentor other personnel, would be helpful for developing the cyber workforce; participants generally said yes. Many also volunteered the opinion that the standard apprentice/master model, in which personnel progress from an apprentice level to a journeyman level to a master level (the traditional 3/5/7-level model for development), was not appropriate for cyber.[69]

Lastly, we asked whether training should focus on other things, in addition to what is currently taught. In 43 percent of discussions, participants said yes and elaborated on what topics

---

[69] For more information about how skill levels are assigned, see Air Force Instruction 36-2101, 2017.

need to be added. These topics included communication, understanding the "why," more about how USAF works, and more about the mission.

## Comments About Merging the 1B4 and 1N4A Career Fields

We did not directly ask participants about the potential merger of the 1B4 and 1N4A career fields, but it was raised by our participants in some discussions. Views on the merger were generally mixed; participants discussed both the pros and the cons. We include these comments in this volume of the report because the merger is under consideration in part because of the similarities in the work that both AFSCs do; if the career fields are similar enough, it could be beneficial for these personnel to be trained in the same way and to be considered interchangeable. However, the merger also has potential implications for retention and recruiting to the extent that personnel have positive or negative attitudes about the merger.

### Merge 1B4 and 1N4A Career Fields

In 23 percent of focus groups, participants volunteered the opinion that the 1B4 and 1N4A career fields should be merged. They expressed the view that the change would better position squadrons to perform their missions and would be more efficient for finding assignment fit and retaining talent.

Some participants talked about the merger possibly providing more opportunities for both career fields.

> I think it is good for the 1B4s as well, because, from my understanding, if they come here, if they don't go through RIOT, then they are very limited to their work roles. They probably wouldn't mind doing some of the stuff we do if they don't mind not being an operator. [1N4A]

> ***

> If we are approved [for the merger], all NSA courses that they run will become available to this workforce as well. This is one of the reasons this merger is appealing. That might be tough to enumerate. [Workforce—other]

> ***

> Training from NSA—what will happen is that it [the merger] won't increase locations where 1B4s are located; it will increase work roles that they can perform in those locations. Right now, airmen go to Fort Meade; if they cannot qualify, there is not much opportunity for them to do anything else. Training there is 12 to 24 months [and] grueling—if they don't make the cut. [There's a] 40-percent success rate in that training. I joke that we suck the least. The problem is that 1Bs get marooned up there—they can't master this training, and then they don't have work roles they can work in. When we combine the career fields, all those work roles that were 1N4 will move over to 1B4, and those 1B4s can then take advantage of the training available for that work role. [Workforce—other]

Another potential benefit of the merger that participants discussed was a reduction in role redundancies and streamlining of organizational structure.

> When you start to put the roles together, we have so many duplicative work roles. . . . Outside a few, like exploit analyst and interactive operators, the two main ones [were] named because, somewhere between 2012 and 2014, we created some chart that said, "If it is an interactive [operation], it is a 1B4, and, if it's exploit, it's a 1N4A." There [are] always other work roles that come online, like planners, access network [operations], different things that both career fields are doing. Pretty much every job that a 1B4 does requires analysis. [Workforce— other]

## Keep 1B4 and 1N4A Career Fields Separate

The idea of the career-field merger was not universally popular, and the possible change was debated during focus group discussions. In 13 percent of focus groups, participants expressed the view that the fields should not be merged. The negative comments ranged from lukewarm to staunchly opposed. A 1B4 equivocated, saying,

> There are benefits to both. I think merging helps give us the perspective of what our counterparts are doing. I just think it's going to muddy the water and it's going to hurt the retention problem. [1B4]

Participants' concerns about the merger centered on the fit of future responsibilities for their interests and skill sets. Participants expressed the view that the merger might contribute to the departure of current airmen who have concerns about what their role will look like moving forward.

> You are going to lose SNCOs because folks like me, you have to get certs when we become a 1B4. We've never been trained to have to do certs. I hope we have the choice, because I may become a bravo again. I'll be like, "Goodbye, alpha! I'm going to go do bravo, where I actually have a clue what I am doing." [1N4A]

Others raised concerns about whether personnel already through the initial training pipeline will have the expertise needed to fulfill the functions of the merged career fields.

> The merger kind of has some uncertainty on fulling intel roles that alphas do. I don't know if 1B4s are fully capable of knowing that intel requirement, because it wasn't in our training. It was a small part in 7-level upgrade training, but it's something that 1B4 will be ill-equipped to take over. [1B4]

# Appendix D. Focus Group Results, by Specialty

In Figures D.1 through D.7, we present the percentage of discussions in which specific comments were mentioned for each of our target specialty groups: 1B4s, 1N4As, and CMF civilians. We note again that group sample sizes reported in these figures are small for the 1N4As ($n = 8$) and especially so for the civilians ($n = 4$). As a result, any differences between the groups should be viewed with great caution. That is, any differences might appear large in the figure, but they might in fact be insignificant, both statistically and practically, in any or all cases.

For example, having only four discussions with civilians means that a difference of one group making or not making a particular point translates to a difference in 25 percent of the groups. If a topic was mentioned in one group, it equates to 25 percent in the figure; if it was mentioned by two, it equates to 50 percent; three equates to 75 percent; and four equates to 100 percent. By contrast, a difference of one group in the 1B4 discussions equates to a difference of only 6 percent. This means that, for the civilian data, it would be an overinterpretation of the data to suggest that something mentioned by four groups (100 percent) is a more widely held view than something mentioned by only three (75 percent). Because the sample is so small, we also cannot conclude that, if something was not mentioned in any of the four groups (0 percent), it is not a concern for civilians.

Lastly, although the total numbers of *groups* are four, eight, and 18 for civilians, 1N4As, and 1B4s, respectively, it is important to note that the numbers of participants in each group are larger (overall participant numbers are seven, 23, and 45, respectively). Although this helps lend additional strength to the data, the number of individuals in the civilian groups are still small, and, for that reason, our caveats above (and elsewhere in this report) still stand.

## Figure D.1. Comments About Training Gaps, by Specialty

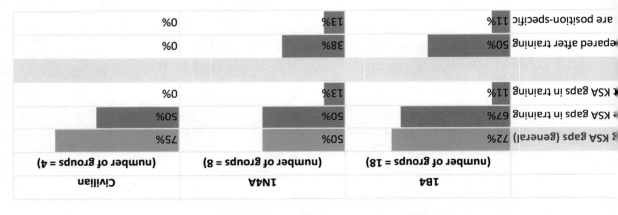

| | 1B4 (number of groups = 18) | 1N4A (number of groups = 8) | Civilian (number of groups = 4) |
|---|---|---|---|
| …g KSA gaps (general) | 72% | 50% | 75% |
| …e KSA gaps in training | 67% | 50% | 50% |
| …t KSA gaps in training | 11% | 13% | 0% |
| …epared after training | 50% | 38% | 0% |
| …are position-specific | 11% | 13% | 0% |

number of focus groups in which a topic was mentioned by at least one person.

raised by one person, and an opposite view was expressed by someone in the same discussion group. In those cases, the [...] n both the topic frequency and the opposite sentiment frequency. For some topics, no opposite sentiment was expressed in the [...] an opposite sentiment was expressed in 3 to 7 percent of the total workforce focus groups (i.e., one or two groups), the category is [...] ntages represent the number of focus groups in which a topic was mentioned by at least one person.

| | 1B4 (number of groups = 18) | 1N4A (number of groups = 8) | Civilian (number of groups = 4) |
|---|---|---|---|
| problems with training and development (general) | 100% | 100% | 100% |
| Training is inapplicable or irrelevant | 83% | 75% | 50% |
| Lack of access to training | 67% | 88% | 75% |
| Lack/poor quality of other resources | 61% | 38% | 75% |
| Length of training or the pipeline is not appropriate* | 61% | 50% | 50% |
| Certain necessary training does not exist | 50% | 63% | 75% |
| ...ing or other resources do not evolve quickly enough* | 50% | 63% | 50% |
| Training doesn't capture the "why"* | 44% | 25% | 50% |
| There are not enough simulations* | 44% | 25% | 25% |
| ...drons are designing unit training and this is a problem | 44% | 25% | 25% |
| Current instruction methods are ineffective | 39% | 25% | 25% |
| Issues with course approval/training design process | 39% | 25% | 25% |
| Skills atrophy after training | 33% | 25% | 25% |
| Training redundancy* | 33% | 25% | 25% |
| Breadth of current training is a problem | 39% | 0% | 25% |
| Air Force does not have proper ownership of training | 28% | 38% | 0% |
| ...quirements ignore airmen's current skill background | 28% | 0% | 25% |
| Cross-training presents challenges* | 33% | 0% | 0% |
| Development path is ambiguous | 6% | 25% | 25% |
| ...te Sentiment: Training is inapplicable or irrelevant | 44% | 25% | 25% |
| Opposite Sentiment: Lack of access to training | 17% | 13% | 25% |
| ...te Sentiment: Lack/poor quality of other resources | 22% | 13% | 0% |
| ...ment: Current instruction methods are ineffective | 17% | 13% | 0% |

**Figure D.2. Views on What Needs to Be Improved in Training, by Specialty**

**Figure D.3. Workforce's Suggested Training Solutions and Changes, by Specialty**

| | 1B4 (number of groups = 18) | 1N4A (number of groups = 8) | Civilian (number of groups = 4) |
|---|---|---|---|
| Improvements or Solutions (general) | 94% | 100% | 100% |
| s or live red forces would be beneficial | 89% | 88% | 100% |
| nds on training/experiential is needed | 83% | 100% | 75% |
| raining per skillset would be beneficial | 56% | 63% | 50% |
| ther military services is a good idea** | 44% | 38% | 75% |
| ptitude testing to help with screening* | 11% | 88% | 25% |
| aining should be structured differently | 33% | 25% | 25% |
| ership of training would be beneficial* | 28% | 25% | 50% |
| ic training options would be beneficial | 33% | 13% | 25% |
| OCO & DCO should be taught to all* | 22% | 38% | 25% |
| ed instructors would improve training | 22% | 13% | 50% |
| 1N4A career fields should be merged | 6% | 75% | 0% |
| p 1B4s & 1N4As separate career fields | 11% | 25% | 0% |
| ations or live reds would be beneficial | 17% | 0% | 25% |

ed by one person, and an opposite view was expressed by someone in the same discussion group. In those cases, the same
th the topic frequency and the opposite sentiment frequency. For some topics, no opposite sentiment was expressed in the
pposite sentiment was expressed in 3 to 7 percent of the total workforce focus groups (i.e., one or two groups), the category is
opposite sentiment was expressed by 10 percent of total focus groups (i.e., three groups), the category is marked with two
he number of focus groups in which a topic was mentioned by at least one person.

**Figure D.4. Views on KSAOs Needed Prior to Entering the Training Pipeline, by Specialty**

| | 1B4 (number of groups = 18) | 1N4A (number of groups = 8) | Civilian (number of groups = 4) |
|---|---|---|---|
| KSAOs Needed Prior to Training* | 78% | 88% | 100% |
| or being a self-starter/self-learner | 56% | 75% | 0% |
| Computer/technical skills | 56% | 25% | 50% |
| Critical thinking or problem solving | 33% | 38% | 75% |
| Ability to learn | 22% | 50% | 25% |

opposite sentiment was expressed in the workforce discussions. Where an opposite sentiment was expressed in 3 to 7 percent of the i.e., one or two groups), the category is marked with an asterisk. Percentages represent the number of focus groups in which a topic person.

**D.5. Other Comments Captured, Unrelated to Recruitment, Retention, or Training, by Specialty**

| | 1B4 (number of groups = 18) | 1N4A (number of groups = 8) | Civilian (number of groups = 4) |
|---|---|---|---|
| Other comments (general)* | 89% | 88% | 50% |
| n keyboard (related to career progression only) | 67% | 63% | 25% |
| personnel are misutilized or ineffectively utilized | 33% | 63% | 50% |
| owledge gap is created when airmen are moved | 28% | 0% | 50% |
| There is a pressure to self-train | 28% | 13% | 0% |
| Retention data are misrepresented/misleading | 22% | 13% | 0% |
| Issues with leadership | 17% | 25% | 0% |
| Pay equity issues | 11% | 25% | 0% |

posite sentiment was expressed in the workforce discussions. Where an opposite sentiment was expressed in 3 to 7 percent of the e., one or two groups), the category is marked with an asterisk. Percentages represent the number of focus groups in which a topic person.

## Figure D.6. Views on Washout Rates, by Specialty

| | 1B4 (number of groups = 18) | | 1N4A (number of groups = 8) | | Civilian (number of groups = 4) | |
|---|---|---|---|---|---|---|
| nts about washout rates (general) | 89% | | 88% | | 75% | |
| rrent washout rates are acceptable | 56% | | 38% | | 25% | |
| Bar for training should be higher | 28% | | 25% | | 0% | |
| ere are currently no washout rates | 11% | | 0% | | 0% | |
| Bar for training should be lower | 6% | | 0% | | 25% | |
| ates that do not express an opinion | 22% | | 25% | | 25% | |

number of focus groups in which a topic was mentioned by at least one person.

## igure D.7. Views on Specific Goals for and Approaches to Training, by Specialty

| | 1B4 (number of groups = 18) | | 1N4A (number of groups = 8) | | Civilian (number of groups = 4) | |
|---|---|---|---|---|---|---|
| Comments about training goals (general) | 83% | | 100% | | 100% | |
| g should be both task and mission focused | 50% | | 88% | | 50% | |
| :or/mentee model would improve training | 61% | | 63% | | 50% | |
| focus on other things not currently taught | 33% | | 63% | | 50% | |
| :chnical capabilities should be a main goal* | 50% | | 25% | | 0% | |
| :ither be task or mission focused, not both | 28% | | 50% | | 25% | |
| The 3/5/7 skill level model is ineffective* | 28% | | 25% | | 0% | |
| :or/mentee model would improve training | 22% | | 13% | | 25% | |

te sentiment was expressed in the workforce discussions. Where an opposite sentiment was expressed in 3 to 7 percent of the
ne or two groups), the category is marked with an asterisk. Percentages represent the number of focus groups in which a topic
son.

110

# Appendix E. Insights from Cyber Training Stakeholders and Subject-Matter Experts

In an effort to capture a wide variety of perspectives in the cyber community, we held 12 discussions with individuals from various organizations that are relevant to the cyber career fields of interest (e.g., the career-field managers, representatives of Air University Cyber College, CyberWorx, and the commander of the 39th Information Operations Squadron). Table E.1 lists the titles of the SMEs and their relevance as an SME or a training stakeholder.

Note that, although our SME list was inclusive of a wide variety of key 1B4 roles, the 1N4A community was not so comprehensively represented. More specifically, interviewees did not include the 1N4 career-field manager, the 316th Training Squadron (which conducts 1N4X1A training), or the 316th Training Squadron Detachment 1 (which oversees JCAC students and serves as liaison between USAF and JCAC training personnel).[70]

**Table E.1. U.S. Air Force Cyber Subject-Matter Expert Interviewees**

| Types of Subject-Matter Expert and Stakeholder Discussions and Titles of Participants | Description |
|---|---|
| Career-field managers | |
|     1B Career-Field Manager (former) | Manages the 1B4 career field |
|     1B Career-Field Manager (current); 1B Deputy Career-Field Manager | Manages the 1B4 career field |
|     Civilian Career-Field Manager; Civilian Force Management Specialist | Manages the civilian cyber personnel |
|     1N4 Deputy Career-Field Manager | Manages the 1N4 career field |
|     17X Career-Field Manager | Manages the 17X officer career field |
| Cyber training experts | |
|     Air Force CyberWorx, U.S. Air Force Academy | Conducts studies examining cyber challenges and provides recommendations for addressing them |
|     Air University Cyber College | Teaches courses on cyber |
|     39th Information Operations Squadron Commander | Provides advanced information operations and cyberspace training for the USAF training pipeline |
|     333rd Training Squadron Commander | Provides officer cyberspace IST and enlisted cyberspace advanced skills training |

---

[70] These SMEs were not among those nominated for inclusion by our sponsor's office, and, therefore, we did not include them in our effort. However, the 1N4 career-field manager who reviewed our report after its completion suggested that these were important personnel to include. Therefore, this represents a gap in the viewpoints expressed in this study, and we note that these individuals might have additional insights worth exploring.

| Types of Subject-Matter Expert and Stakeholder Discussions and Titles of Participants | Description |
|---|---|
| 333rd Training Squadron Instructors and Curriculum Developer | Delivers training and develops curriculum |
| ACC and 24th Air Force Cyber Workforce Leaders | |
| Deputy Director, Cyberspace and Information Dominance Headquarters/Air Combat Command; and six others at Langley Air Force Base | Many 24th Air Force (Air Forces Cyber) cyber personnel are stationed at Langley Air Force Base under the oversight of ACC |
| Executive Director, 24th Air Force | Recommended by another SME for insights into training for civilians in the CMF within 24th Air Force. The executive director oversees the readiness of both enlisted and civilians. |

Each discussion was unique and tailored to the individual's role and relevance as an SME or stakeholder. For example, we asked participants to provide us with background on their organization and their role, insights they might have from that vantage point that might be relevant to the study goals, and an overview of key topics in their domain (e.g., we asked career-field managers to clarify aspects of the current training pipelines and to direct us to documents that might be relevant for us to review). We also asked a few of the same types of questions that we did of the cyber workforce members; however, we did not go through the whole protocol.

As mentioned in the main body of this report, views shared by SMEs were not seemingly different from the views of relevant workforce members. However, we gained interesting insights into the state of the cyber field, which we briefly discuss in the next section.

Overall, SME discussions provided us with more information about the career fields of interest, including details about the training pipelines, thoughts on recruitment and retention, and ideas about how to improve the training and development of cyber personnel. In general, SMEs expressed similar sentiments as members of the workforce, with few cases in which there were conflicting perspectives. In some cases, SMEs shared unique perspectives. A summary of key themes that emerged from these discussions is provided below.

## Some Insights from the Subject-Matter Expert Discussions

Like the members of the workforce, the SMEs acknowledged that there is room for improvement in training, and some expressed a view that major improvements are needed. For example, one SME talked about the importance of improving training and retention of the best and brightest but expressed concern that training needs might continue to go unaddressed and even unnoticed.

> People say we need a cyber Pearl Harbor before it gets attention, and actually realize what is happening in this domain. But we have had several Pearl Harbors, and people didn't seem to mind—for example, OPM [the U.S. Office of Personnel Management] [was] hacked, and all personal data was stolen. We still don't know where it went or what they are doing with it, but people are like, "Eh, it just happens. Nothing blew up or caught on fire, and everyone is still eating,

so, no big deal." My big concern is that, in future conflicts, things we have glossed over may really haunt us.

Several SMEs, in addition to members of the workforce, pointed to the challenge associated with maintaining training currency, highlighting that technology is evolving more quickly than USAF is able to develop training. For example, one SME mentioned that USAF often obtains new equipment and programs but does not account for the funds needed to train the workforce on the new equipment. However, another SME noted that the perception that military cyber training is not evolving as quickly as nonmilitary cyber training is more problematic.

> There is an internal perception that AETC is slow, their process is slow in curriculum updating, and it's slow and it's industrial age to keep up with the modern fight. There is some truth to that. But, for me, the concern is the perspective itself. . . . The perception of slowness in cyber training, it leads people to think they will never get this done and then they have to do it themselves. This then introduces a problem where we are taking people who should probably be on mission, and they are building training. Developing curriculum does take time, especially when you are building it on the backs of instructors. But I don't think we are quite as crappy as what people think we are. But maybe I am blinded by our own optimism.

Some SMEs mentioned the challenges associated with bringing the right personnel into the cyber career field and said that efforts are underway to enhance screening assessments to better identify personnel with the right aptitude to perform cyber-related work, but none of these efforts are complete, and no assessments are in place yet.

Some SMEs said that USAF needs to tailor training toward the individual needs of the airmen instead of relying on the one-size-fits-all model that is currently in use. One SME noted,

> You have a cohort of students who begin and finish together. In that cohort, you have a wide variety of ability. . . . Right now, we're doing one size fits all. . . . The students who already [understand] the material are now bored, and you're struggling to keep them engaged. How do I train at various rates and get them what they need, instead of a cookie-cutter approach? . . . It goes back to individualized learning. I am a big fan of it, but the military doesn't do anything individualized. We're this big giant mass of people in green uniforms being marched through a pipeline. That's how the military approaches learning in general.

When asked how to incorporate individualized training, the same SME made the following suggestion:

> You chunk [training content] into smaller pieces of discrete technologies. You then provide [training content] in a way folks can get to at any point in their career. If my class now covers a block on Windows, Linux, exploitation, whatever . . . they can take that block rather than go through the entire pipeline. Right now, it doesn't support that. We need that.

113

Building on these ideas, another SME discussed the potential benefits of implementing an online marketplace for airmen to exchange ideas and access training materials and tying this system to talent management. Specifically,

> I think there is a value of linking [an online marketplace] with talent management where I can see that, if Joe Bob is really good at something, I can use that to manage him and say, "Here are some places you can go where we can use you to the best." If you look at training and see how it mingles with talent management, I don't think they are separable topics; I don't think you can do talent management minus training. It's workforce development. I think talent management and training need to be linked.

Likewise, other SMEs informed us of an adaptive learning system that is currently being considered to assist in providing training on demand.

> From a mission defense team perspective, we are trying to create [an] adaptive learning environment, so everyone can get a license, and, depending [on] what your work role is, you would have a training plan geared towards that. If you are a software developer, you can go and do this and get training that gets you going, and, sooner or later, you will have to get off of that [learning system] and get hands-on training. In some cases, we have been looking into engaging and hands-on training to some extent. We are trying to improve; instead of sending a cast of a thousand out to a training course away from their job, they are able to get it when they want it. It's like training on demand.

***

> Some of the training platforms, at least one that we were looking at, [were] adaptive, so you would take a test or quiz to ascertain where your skill level is at, and then the system would adapt based off of that for what training to provide to you. Through the training, there are more small quizzes to kind of see if you are understanding and see if you are doing good and ready to move onto the next.

Although SMEs and members of the workforce shared similar perceptions, there were a few specific instances in which opposing views surfaced. Specifically, in one discussion, an SME stated that USAF should rely on commercial-based training opportunities and that it is not necessary for USAF to take ownership of that training. Although this idea was mentioned by one SME, it is important to highlight because a push to have more USAF-centric training was expressed by members of the workforce. Another minor discrepancy between SMEs and members of the workforce is related to retention challenges. As mentioned in the main body of the report, members of the workforce expressed the belief that there is a retention problem, of which industry competition is a primary driver. One SME said that it would be hard to argue that there is a retention problem when looking at the data, and another stated that there are other drivers of this problem that are greater than pay.

> I don't think that pay is a big driver. There are some people [who] get out because of pay, but most of the people get out for primarily two reasons:
> (1) talent management—they get stuck doing things they hate; [and]
> (2) bureaucratic annoyances—mundane things they should be able to do, they

can't, and they get fed up and leave. That could be admin process, or making their voice feel heard, and they feel like their voice and expertise don't get heard. There are things in the military in cyber that we can do that industry cannot, and that is a huge benefit that we have to counter fight the salary issue. Talent management is completely broken, from both a personal-growth standpoint and knowing what a valuable skill set is.

Similarly, SMEs explained that it is challenging to understand what motivates cyber personnel to leave the service, because the career field does not have a way to consistently track and monitor where personnel who leave go and why.

Talking about retaining [civilians], we do not do a good job of asking through an exit interview as to why they are leaving. You can look at our career field and say we lost 100 people and say, "Why did they leave?" Well, we don't know, did they leave gov, or just go to another area? They could go to [the] scientist and engineering career field—they never left the Air Force; they just changed communities. If Joe leaves Federal Service, we don't see that reason for why they are leaving. We are actually trying to answer these questions for our boss; data is not readily available.

Notably, one SME expressed the belief that it would be valuable to investigate cyber personnel motives for staying in the military and hypothesized two primary reasons:

I think it would be interesting to find out and talk to people who got out that are successful in industry and compare that to the people who stay in. I think you will find two types who stayed: those who got lucky and managed in a way that made sense to them, and those who were very risk-averse about changing their job. It would be interesting to tease apart, and I do not know how you would identify those people.

There were also a few cases in which SMEs brought up issues that were not mentioned by members of the workforce. For example, one SME described internal competition within USAF to gain top talent. Specifically,

We compete against other top career fields, and recruiters are tasked with finding the hard [jobs], like PJ [pararescue jumper] and combat controller [or] a Russian linguist. When those young people qualify for any AFSC, we want them, and then that is an internal Air Force competition. We need to change our messaging on targeting and recruiting in terms of incentives that we are able to provide, [like] service credit, etc., trying to establish what can get people additional credit or advanced degrees, trying to make that available to recruiters so they know what they can sell.

There were some other unique discussion points; one SME mentioned that previous aircraft maintainers are particularly successful in cyber compared with other cross-trained airmen, another suggested that aptitude screening should also be used in hiring civilians, and some SMEs suggested using a competency tracking system to reward airmen. Specifically,

Look at how we do pro-pay for lawyers and doctors, and, to be honest, I have looked at applying that across the enlisted force as well. Or the ability to do competencies or things like that. You could probably get away from retention bonuses because it is up to members to keep qualifications for pro-pay. If you hire an attorney and they lose the bar [do not maintain their license to practice law], it is not upon the Air Force to make sure they stay up to par with the bar [complete training to maintain their licensing]. It is on them. I think we could do a similar model in the IT and cyber fields.

Another SME stated,

There should be compensation for how they have garnered skills out of their own pocket. And have some incentive to say, hey, OK, if you have your certification for whatever, that there is some incentive to stay here and utilize [those skills].

Likewise, when we asked SMEs about recruitment and retention problems for civilians, they mentioned that the Cyber Excepted Service is under consideration as a way to better attract and retain the civilian workforce and to handle cases in which cyber personnel express a desire to remain on keyboard rather than be promoted to leadership roles.[71] Finally, one SME offered sentiments related to the measurement of cyber training success, questioning whether cyber training is effective.

I don't think we have any measures to see if our training is effective. How do we measure to see if we are meeting combatant command requirements? You [go to IST first], then go through ACC and then maybe other CYBERCOM training, and how do we know we are being effective? How do we know we are doing the right job across the continuum? . . . Are we really building the right courses? . . . If you aren't getting [training] upstream, then they build it downstream. Who is playing the ringmaster of all the training that is out there? How do we measure the effectiveness of our training enterprise? That's a really big deal.

---

[71] For more information on the Cyber Excepted Service, see Chief Information Officer, U.S. Department of Defense, undated.

# Appendix F. Examples of How Training Does Not Adequately Prepare Personnel for Their Unit Assignments

This appendix provides examples of comments about how training does not adequately prepare personnel for their unit assignments. These types of comments are discussed generally at the start of Chapter 2 and are reported as being mentioned in 40 percent of the discussions in Figure 2.1.

> In general, the training we are given, it's a good starting point, but it never really builds upon itself to help further the cyber skills. I've been through offensive and defensive sides now. CBT specific here as an example, the training we are given to operate our weapons system is training to start it up; that is literally it. There is no training that actually teaches us how to use it properly. We had to use an outside source recently, and that is the only training that I've received from this unit from the CBT construct in whole; that's an outside source that actually covers anything to do with what we work with.

***

> An example of that would be collecting processes on a system, [which] is used to determine if malicious software is running. They might say, "You run this command, and you get these processes." But then you go through the schoolhouse, get to the unit, and now they are like, "You have 800 systems; I need processes on all of them." But you haven't been taught, haven't been explicitly told how to connect all these parts to make something happen to achieve that task. All tasks taught in vacuum.

***

> The missions are so different for each individual that you could be trained for that one thing specifically and then go to a team that doesn't do any of that. Training for what exactly? You can be Air Force–qualified, as far as training goes, but not mission-qualified, and then you go to be mission-qualified, and then that training tells a whole bunch of other stuff that you are just not prepared for or didn't learn anything prior to it or didn't have a good fundamental for. Once you learn it, by the time you get done, three years is up; you are thinking about getting out and moving along.

***

> These are the gaps I have seen coming from OCO; defenders do not have an understanding of the adversary and how they operate; they are mainly being trained from IT perspective, with technology in mind, and how to operate tools. Let's use a law enforcement analogy—the cop tries to catch bank robbers or thieves, and they kind of have to study how they steal things and what tactics they use so they can get ahead of those tactics. But we don't train to understand tactics, we train our defenders to click a button and look at packets, and so there is a major disconnect when talking about capabilities that the defenders have. They see information and the data, but they don't see how and why the adversary

117

wants to come in [and] steal it right under their nose. They see the information and data but don't understand why an adversary would want to steal it. That is the biggest gap to me. There are probably budget issues, and they want to get training concise. They come from a place where tech is the most important, not the adversary. When they built the training, they did not realize how important it was.

\*\*\*

I wouldn't say it is the amount of training, per se, but it is quality of training. We spend weeks and weeks and weeks teaching people how to drop a bomb correctly, but cyber can be weaponized just as easily if we teach people to think differently. Here is training that makes you think differently, apply this as a weapons system. Take a cyber weapons course, and do it on a real range. Teach people to think about war. Let's weaponize it. Learn how to practice like you play. Only a few jobs actually allow you to get that experience. We want these people to be cyber warriors who are constantly ready to defend and attack. That should be the mindset of everyone—that you are using cyber as a weapon, not just pushing a button. You are defending like cops at the base. Every cop at the base is prepared to defend.

\*\*\*

The curriculum has changed since when I went through the schoolhouse and follow-on training, but there definitely was a lack when I was going through. It felt like they were just giving a brief overview of what our actual position here working as a CBT would actually be doing; it was just a brief overview of what tools we would be using and the barest minimum of how to use them in CWO, which is IQT.

\*\*\*

A lot of these civilian side certifications and things like that, a lot of those models, don't apply to how the military applies cyber in an actual environment. They don't have the bureaucracy that we have to go through. They can get from point A to B going through a network or whatever their objective is, and that is how they teach you within the confines of the class, but, due to the restrictions placed on us by authorities, by the agency, but a lot of that is not necessarily a one-for-one application. Yeah, certain concepts that are taught within the courses are applicable to what we would do. However, the steps we would do are definitely not one-for-one. So, some of the classes, you do need to be very picky.

\*\*\*

I think when you talk about former training, you do not get what you need out of Keesler or CWO [IQT]. They are both outdated and don't apply to most of what people here do. Enlisted aren't taught to plan. But we will take a guy and tell him to go do it and tell him to do it. I am not prepared for this. We don't do a good job of keeping the courses up to date.

\*\*\*

It'd be like if you took someone who spent their life working on a certain type of car and brought them to work on a completely different type of vehicle. It's completely different.

\*\*\*

For someone who just started DCO, they are not going to be as trained as someone who ended up doing OCO right out of tech school. After tech school, someone doing OCO will be in school for another two years to learn OCO stuff, versus who is in tech—"Hey, we will give you a few more weeks, and off you go." You get roughly two years more training if you are OCO.

***

For IQT—it is just to give you a basic well-rounded view of what you may do. It is really what comes after where the problems are. You have a really specific CPT [cyber protection team] to be trained on, and so you have a pre-course and a course based on your weapon [system]. And that gap is so wide we send ops there and they come back and we have to retrain. They were designed to send them, get qualified, and ready for mission. That is 100 percent not the case. When I went down three years ago, I went through the course, learned basic skills, came here. The first few courses, new concepts were introduced. And the main thing that I remember, they are like, "Hey, congrats, you guys are going through advanced-level forensics course." And I was like, "Well, great, I have never done beginners'-level forensics course." I had no idea what my job here at the squad—we do not do forensics, but I used the weapons [system]. I still have no idea why they wasted the money and I got nothing out of it. As far as getting better at my job, it did not do that. The do have a different course now. I just know I was like, "Why would you send me through that course?"

***

So, a couple problems here. There's no way you'd have a pilot show up to a unit who's not qualified, but that's what we see here. So, we get about 80 percent of people from IST who aren't ready, and we have to send them to IQT. We end up shouldering the responsibility to get them prepared. It affects readiness and effectiveness. We're getting operators that are not ready to counter the adversaries we want to counter. We're trying to make up for the lack of training.

***

I have interviewed people when they get out of training, and they still lack fundamental concepts of doing the job.

***

The schools I went to were just production models; 100 students go in, 99 come out, very little failure, with no critical thinking. There is memorization—you throw it up on a test, and then you are done. The other school I went to actually tested you and trained critical thinking; they required you to learn the skills and then apply the skills. If the school is like that now, then I think it's good, but, after that, there is nothing—you just go to your job.

119

# Appendix G. 1B4 and 1N4A Training Courses, Their Owners, and Their Locations in the Training Pipeline

Table G.1 provides an overview of the relevant cyber coursework completed by the 1B4s and 1N4As.

**Table G.1. 1B4 and 1N4A Training Courses**

| Course or Training Event | Relevant U.S. Air Force Specialty | U.S. Air Force Specialty or Work-Role Requirement? | Location in Training Pipeline | Owner |
|---|---|---|---|---|
| JCAC | 1N4X1A | Yes; AFS requirement | IST | NSA |
| CWO | Either | Yes; work-role requirement (multiple) | IQT | ACC |
| SANS | Either | No; commercially available | Intermediate/advanced training | Company (SANS) |
| CISCO | Either | No; commercially available | Intermediate/advanced training | Company (CISCO) |
| CWO Apprentice Course (AC) | 1B4X1 | Yes; AFS requirement | IST | AETC |
| UCT | 1B4X1 in this context | Yes; colloquial but imprecise term for CWO-AC (AFS requirement) | IST (17X), but used in this report to refer to 1B4X1 | AETC |
| Root9B | Either | Partially; commercially available. USAF requirement for supported CYBERCOM work roles within one wing | Intermediate/advanced training | Company (Root9B) |
| CNOQC | Either | Yes; work-role requirement (multiple) | Mission qualification training (course part of RIOT) | NSA |
| Carnegie Mellon | Either | Yes; work-role requirement (work-role training has since been changed) | IQT | Carnegie Mellon |
| RIOT | Either | Yes; work-role requirement | Mission qualification training | NSA |
| Cyber 200 | Either | No | Intermediate training | Air Force Institute of Technology (AFIT) |
| Joint Targeting School Staff Course | Either | Yes; work-role training | Mission qualification training | Joint Staff J7 |
| Cyberspace Vulnerability Assessment/Hunter | Either | Yes; work-role training | IQT | ACC |
| Defense Cyber Investigation Training Academy | Either | Yes; work-role training | IQT | Defense Cyber Crime Center |

| Course or Training Event | Relevant U.S. Air Force Specialty | U.S. Air Force Specialty or Work-Role Requirement? | Location in Training Pipeline | Owner |
|---|---|---|---|---|
| Intermediate Network Warfare Training | Either | Yes; work-role training (predecessor to CWO course) | IQT | Air Force Space Command |
| CYBER3800 | Either | Yes; work-role training | Mission qualification training | NSA |
| GIAC Certified Intrusion Analyst (GCIA) | Either | No; commercially available | Intermediate/advanced training | Company (SANS) |
| Cyber 300 | Either | No | Intermediate training | Air Force Institute of Technology (AFIT) |

SOURCE: Information provided by 1BX career-field manager.

# References

Air Force Instruction 36-2101, *Classifying Military Personnel (Officer and Enlisted)*, Washington, D.C.: Headquarters, Department of the Air Force, March 9, 2017.

Air Force Personnel Center, *Air Force Enlisted Classification Directory (AFECD): The Official Guide to the Air Force Enlisted Classification Codes*, Joint Base San Antonio, Tex., October 31, 2019.

American Educational Research Association, American Psychological Association, and National Council on Measurement in Education, *Standards for Educational and Psychological Testing*, Washington, D.C.: American Educational Research Association, 2014.

Bui, Anh T., "1st Non-Prior Service Airman Graduates CWO Course," U.S. Air Force, April 11, 2019. As of March 31, 2021:
https://www.960cyber.afrc.af.mil/News/Article-Display/Article/1813072/1st-non-prior-service-airman-graduates-cwo-course/

Chiaramonte, Michael V., Douglas R. Howe, and Jeffrey A. Collins, *A 21st Century Training Model for Flexible, Quick, and Life-Long Workforce Development*, United States Air Force Academy, Colo.: Air Force CyberWorx, Report 16-001, 2016.

Chief Information Officer, U.S. Department of Defense, "DoD Cyber Excepted Service (CES) Personnel System," webpage, undated. As of March 31, 2021:
https://dodcio.defense.gov/Cyber-Workforce/CES.aspx

Hardison, Chaitra M., Leslie Adrienne Payne, John A. Hamm, Angela Clague, Jacqueline Torres, David Schulker, and John S. Crown, *Attracting, Recruiting, and Retaining Successful Cyberspace Operations Officers: Cyber Workforce Interview Findings*, Santa Monica, Calif.: RAND Corporation, RR-2618-AF, 2019. As of March 31, 2021:
https://www.rand.org/pubs/research_reports/RR2618.html

Hardison, Chaitra M., Leslie Adrienne Payne, Julia Whitaker, Anthony Lawrence, and Ivica Pavisic, *Building the Best Offensive and Defensive Cyber Workforce*: Volume II, *Attracting and Retaining Enlisted and Civilian Personnel*, Santa Monica, Calif.: RAND Corporation, RR-A1056-2, 2021.

Montes, Alexandre, "Intelligence Exploitation Analysts: Creating Cyberspace Warriors," U.S. Air Force, April 17, 2017. As of February 4, 2020:
https://www.16af.af.mil/News/Legacy/Article/1153488/intelligence-exploitation-analysts-creating-cyberspace-warriors/

Morris, Jeffrey D., and Frederick R. Waage, *Cyber Aptitude Assessment—Finding the Next Generation of Enlisted Cyber Soldiers*, West Point, N.Y.: Army Cyber Institute, 2012.

Newhouse, William, Stephanie Keith, Benjamin Scribner, and Gregory Witte, *National Initiative for Cybersecurity Education (NICE) Cybersecurity Workforce Framework*, Gaithersburg, Md.: National Institute of Standards and Technology, NIST Special Publication 800-181, August 2017.

Nye, Christopher D., Fritz Drasgow, Oleksandr S. Chernyshenko, Stephen Stark, U. Christean Kubisiak, Leonard A. White, and Irwin Jose, *Assessing the Tailored Adaptive Personality Assessment System (TAPAS) as an MOS Qualification Instrument*, Ft. Belvoir, Va.: U.S. Army Research Institute for the Behavioral and Social Sciences, Technical Report 1312, August 2012. As of July 29, 2021:
https://apps.dtic.mil/sti/pdfs/ADA566090.pdf

Robbert, Albert A., Michael G. Mattock, Beth J. Asch, John S. Crown, James Hosek, and Tara L. Terry, *Supplemental Career Paths for Air Force Pilots: A Warrant Officer Component or an Aviation Technical Track?* Santa Monica, Calif.: RAND Corporation, RR-2617-AF, 2018. As of April 2, 2021:
https://www.rand.org/pubs/research_reports/RR2617.html

Society for Industrial and Organizational Psychology, *Principles for the Validation and Use of Personnel Selection Procedures*, 4th ed., Bowling Green, Ohio, 2003.

Theohary, Catherine A., *Defense Primer: Cyberspace Operations*, Washington, D.C.: Congressional Research Service, IF10537, Version 3, last updated December 18, 2018.

———, *Defense Primer: Cyberspace Operations*, Washington, D.C.: Congressional Research Service, IF10537, Version 4, last updated December 15, 2020.

Trippe, D. Matthew, Karen O. Moriarty, Teresa L. Russell, Thomas R. Carretta, and Adam S. Beatty, "Development of a Cyber/Information Technology Knowledge Test for Military Enlisted Technical Training Qualification," *Military Psychology*, Vol. 26, No. 3, 2014, pp. 182–198.

U.S. Government Accountability Office, *DOD Training: U.S. Cyber Command and Services Should Take Actions to Maintain a Trained Cyber Mission Force*, Washington, D.C., GAO-19-362, March 2019.

Weggeman, Chris P., "Military Cyber Programs and Posture," presentation to the U.S. Senate Armed Services Committee Subcommittee on Cybersecurity, Washington, D.C.: U.S. Senate, March 13, 2018.